SHENSO **CONSULTING**

D0356502

SHENSON ON CONSULTING

Success Strategies from the "Consultant's Consultant"

HOWARD L. SHENSON, CMC

John Wiley & Sons
New York ● Chichester ● Brisbane ● Toronto ● Singapore

Library of Congress Cataloging in Publication Data:

Shenson, Howard L.
    Shenson on consulting : success strategies from the consultant's
consultant / Howard L. Shenson.
        p.   cm.
    Includes bibliographical references.
    ISBN 0-471-50661-3 (cloth)
    ISBN 0-471-00925-3 (paper)
    1. Consultants.   I. Title.
HD69.C6S519   1990
001'.068—dc20   90-30240

Printed in the United States of America

10   9   8   7   6   5   4   3   2   1

To my parents,
Hermine and Sidney Shenson,
a great source of
motivation and encouragement

ACKNOWLEDGMENTS

This book would never have been possible were it not for the stimulating and thought-provoking questions of thousands of participants in my seminars, subscribers to my newsletter, and clients. I am indebted to their curiosity and to the creative editing of Tiffany Jordan.

CONTENTS

*If I am really one of the best professionals in my field, do I need to market
my services? o Which is more important for success, marketing or
technical competence? o How much of my time should be devoted to
marketing? o What marketing strategies are used by the most successful
consultants and professionals? o What are the prime reasons consulting
practices fail? o What are the early warning signs that my practice may
be in trouble? o How greatly will the name I select for my practice affect*

my chances for success?   ○   *What information should be included on my business card?*   ○   *Should I use a résumé to promote my services?*   ○   *Are brokers effective for securing new clients?*   ○   *Should I promote my consulting services to corporate personnel departments?*   ○   *Should I ever recommend other consultants or professionals to potential clients? Does it ever pay to promote my competitors?*   ○   *Can responding to help-wanted ads produce consulting business?*   ○   *Does it pay for my professional firm to be listed in directories?*   ○   *Is networking really a profitable use of my time?*   ○   *Will contacting past friends and associates produce significant business?*   ○   *How can I effectively promote my services to previous business and professional contacts?*   ○   *How can I get an appointment with the high-level prospects that I really want to see?*   ○   *Do club memberships produce business?*   ○   *How can I make my name a household word with potential prospects or clients?*   ○   *How can I encourage the press to publicize my services?*   ○   *How can I use public speaking engagements to promote my professional services?*   ○   *How can I identify public-speaking opportunities?*   ○   *Is giving seminars a viable means of building my professional image and marketing my services?*   ○   *What are the benefits of publishing a newsletter?*   ○   *How do I develop and publish a newsletter?*   ○   *Will selling information products have a negative impact on my professional image?*

3   REFERRAL MARKETING: MAKING YOUR PRACTICE GROW THROUGH REFERRALS AND RECOMMENDATIONS

What tactics can I use to stimulate follow-on business and referrals?   ○   *What's the best way to act on a referral from a client?*   ○   *What percentage of my business can I expect to generate from referrals?*   ○   *How can I ensure that 80 percent of new business comes from referrals?*   ○   *Should I give gifts as thanks for referrals?*

4   DIRECT MARKETING: USING ADVERTISING AND BROCHURES TO PROMOTE YOUR PRACTICE

Won't advertising my services create the impression that I'm in need of business and unsuccessful?   ○   *Can "cold" direct mail promotion really produce clients?*   ○   *How profitable is it to follow up direct mail promotions to prospects with telemarketing?*   ○   *Should I write my own brochure or retain a professional to do so?*   ○   *What information should be included in a brochure or capabilities statement?*   ○   *Which should I do first—design my brochure or write the copy?*   ○   *How can I get my brochure in the hands of viable prospects?*   ○   *Do newspaper or magazine ads produce clients?*   ○   *Should my ad be general or highly specific?*   ○   *How can I increase the pulling power of my advertising?*   ○   *How can I measure the results achieved by my advertising?*   ○   *How can I test the effectiveness of my marketing communications?* ○ *How can I test an ad or direct mail promotion inexpensively?*

How can I avoid appearing too anxious when I need the business? ○ *Should I tell prospects about my past clients?* ○ *How do I provide references if I'm new to private practice or am providing services in a new area of specialty?* ○ *How should I respond to a request for references?* ○ *How can I prevent potential clients from pressing me to work for them full-time?* ○ *How can I serve small clients unable to afford my fee?* ○ *How do I remain fresh and creative when selling a service I have sold many times?* ○ *Does being controlling and assertive with clients always help?* ○ *In the first meeting with a prospect, how do I get control of the encounter?* ○ *How do I regain control in the initial meeting with a prospective client?* ○ *How can I get prospects to recognize the value of my skills and experience?* ○ *How can I keep prospects from wasting my time?* ○ *How can I ensure that marketing time isn't wasted by underlings not able to commit for my services?* ○ *What are some good questions to ask to quickly get a handle on the client's needs?* ○ *What questions, even if not asked, should I be sure to answer when selling my services?* ○ *What are the principal fears a client is likely to have about retaining my services?* ○ *Will telling my client the blunt truth ever hurt my business?* ○ *What face-to-face selling strategies have professionals found most effective?* ○ *What strategies work best when selling my services to a committee or board?* ○ *How do I evaluate the effectiveness of my face-to-face selling skills?* ○ *How can I avoid giving away valuable services for free?* ○ *How should I handle requests for free services from friends, relatives, or colleagues?* ○ *Should I exchange services with other professionals?* ○ *How do I deal with efforts by the client's staff to torpedo my success?* ○ *Will turning down business hurt my image?* ○ *What are some simple, low-cost ways to stimulate additional business from existing clients?* ○ *How can I make myself indispensable to clients?* ○ *How can I obtain publicity for successful accomplishments for clients?*

How should my services be priced? ○ *Is it better to work for a fixed price or for a daily or hourly rate?* ○ *Is working on a retainer advantageous?*

○ *What's the best way to obtain a start-up payment or front-end retainer from a new client?* ○ *What percentage of the fee can be obtained prior to delivery of services?* ○ *Should I ever cut my fee to get the business?* ○ *To what extent will increasing my fee result in my losing clients and business?* ○ *Should I charge indirect expenses separately or include them in my fee?* ○ *How should I charge for travel expenses?* ○ *Is it possible to charge for travel time?* ○ *Does conducting a feasibility study for a client generally result in additional business?* ○ *Should I provide my prospect with a proposal even when not specifically asked for one?* ○ *How can I make my proposal stand out from those of my competitors?* ○ *Is it advantageous to combine a proposal and contract?* ○ *Is a written agreement with my client always necessary?* ○ *Should I require clients to sign a contract for a short consultation?* ○ *Should I have a hold harmless clause in my contract?* ○ *How frequently should I invoice my clients?* ○ *Will progress reports assist me in being paid in a timely fashion?* ○ *How can I avoid the requirement of having to write a final report?* ○ *Is there any information that should be excluded from a written (final) report?* ○ *How can I find time to do really creative work with all of the daily interruptions?* ○ *How can I find time to respond promptly to calls and letters?* ○ *Is it preferable to use an answering service, an answering machine, or a voice mail system?* ○ *How do solo practices compare financially to larger professional service firms?*

INTRODUCTION

Professional consulting—providing advice and information in exchange for a fee—is one of the fastest-growing segments of the economy. Many persons engaged in consulting don't, of course, call themselves consultants. They have adopted other titles—financial planner, accountant, attorney, trainer, consulting engineer, psychologist, advisor, architect, designer, etc. Regardless of what they call themselves, however, they are linked by the need to identify a client, package their know-how into a saleable service, deliver advice and information in a fashion that satisfies the needs of the client, and be compensated in relation to the value of their time or service. Marketing professional consulting services is unique. It is fundamentally different from marketing products. Indeed, it is even distinct from the methods employed for the marketing of other types of services. Those who are able to master the art and science of marketing professional practice not only benefit economically, but enjoy a level of personal satisfaction that is usually the envy of their less successful peers and of others.

Some professional consultants mistakenly think that just being good at what they do is sufficient to build and maintain a profitable practice. Others are shackled by the feeling that marketing is beneath them or somehow unprofessional. Selecting and implementing incorrect or inappropriate marketing strategies can destroy a professional firm. But so too can avoiding the necessity of marketing.

Those not familiar with private practice often believe that professionals are universally prosperous. They view all, or almost all, lawyers, financial planners, attorneys, medical doctors, business consultants, architects, etc., as highly successful and financially well off. Research clearly demonstrates that this is not the case. Success in private practice is not evenly distributed. The classic bell-shaped curve

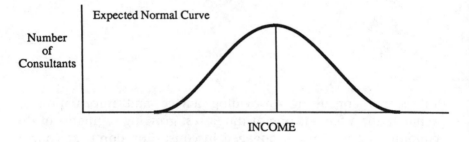

does not mirror reality. Instead, success is bimodal. While there are a vast number of highly successful professionals, there are an even greater number just getting by. The following is a far more accurate depiction of professional success.

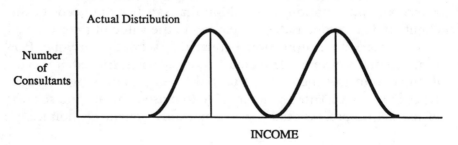

Unlike the general public, most professionals are well aware of this dichotomy. But many fail to understand the reason behind it. The evidence is very clear. The distinction between the successful and the not so successful is not a function of technical or professional expertise, education (having attended the right school), or luck. Skill in marketing and selling, more than any other factor, explains the difference between those who struggle and those who flourish at the pinnacle of success.

Shenson on Consulting is designed to provide the reader with detailed, research-based strategies for effective marketing of professional consulting services. It indicates what works and why. Of equal importance, it specifies strategies that should be avoided because they are either unprofessional and damaging or ineffective. Much of the information is communicated through answers to the 97 most frequently asked (important) questions about how to build and maintain a profitable practice. These questions, from practicing professionals, have been carefully researched. The answers are not theoretical, but specific and strategic.

This book is designed to be read in two ways, both of which are recommended. First, it should be read in its entirety—cover to cover. Doing so will provide perspective and communicate the book's important underlying philosophy. Then, as specific marketing and selling concerns and opportunities arise, the reader should study the answers to particular questions.

Make no mistake, the proper selection and effective implementation of professional practice marketing strategies and tactics will have a material impact on the success of your practice.

SHENSON ON CONSULTING

1

THIRTEEN KEYS:
Building and Maintaining
a Successful
Consulting Practice

Building a successful consulting practice requires that marketing be based on proper approach, attitude, and underlying philosophy. For a professional, marketing is much more like a carefully orchestrated symphony than a buffet dinner. Irregular and ad hoc implementation of seemingly effective strategies and tactics used by others can be more damaging than helpful. To build and maintain a viable professional firm, marketing must permeate every activity. The successful don't worry about marketing only on Monday or Friday; they worry about it twenty-four hours a day, seven days a week. Every action of the professional has an impact on the acquisition of future business. The professional sells image, technology, knowledge, insight, competence, creativity, attitude, and even philosophical approach. Unlike products or even other services, the work product (professional service) cannot be separated from the delivery vehicle (the professional).

In digesting this book, the reader will discover hundreds of strategies and tactics that have a proven track record for producing success in business development. But borrowing strategies and tactics, however creative, will not result in a viable consulting practice. Whether the marketing strategies are adopted as is or refined and personalized, their effectiveness will be assured only when used within a strategic philosophical context. Now, and as you continue to read, develop a marketing philosophy and stance that will make the selection of appropriate strategies obvious and comfortable, and that will provide a context for practice development that is logical and meaningful for you, your associates, and those you serve.

An awareness of the underlying philosophy and approach of your most successful colleagues will be beneficial. Research clearly indicates that those most successful in marketing professional or consulting services share the following characteristics:

1. A dedication to a market orientation. Ours is a market-driven economy. Those who prosper in the market, including professionals, start with the market and develop services (or products) responsive to market demand. Take care to avoid the practice that has toppled so many who seemed destined for success—creating elegant solutions to nonexistent problems. Always start with the market and work backward. The ability to determine what the market desires through research, testing, or intuition is the most basic and fundamental principle of marketing consulting services.

2. A commitment to target and niche marketing. No consultant can be all things to all clients. Success is a result of carefully defining the services to be provided in terms of market segments. This point is perhaps best illustrated by the following story about a participant in a seminar on marketing professional services.

New to private practice, he planned to set up shop as a marketing consultant. An experienced marketer in the employ of a large manufacturing firm, he informed the seminar leader that he now had to make his most difficult decision—on what and for whom he would consult. He selected a very new but rapidly growing industry. Within three years he had established his firm as the leading marketing authority and resource in this specialized, niche market. He had more business than he could handle, contributed articles to trade magazines serving the industry, gave speeches, conducted seminars, and was regularly contacted by the press for his views on issues regarding this narrow specialty.

The selection of his market niche was, in a sense, accidental; he could have elected to serve a different segment. His success, however, was the result of target and niche marketing. Being good at what he does is important and helpful, but not causal; there are many generalist marketing consultants who are good, though not successful.

3. A devotion to client interest, above and beyond any other. More than anything, clients retain consultants with the assumption (hope) that they will be dedicated to placing the client's interest and well-being above and beyond any other interest, even their own self-interest. For the most successful, this goes far beyond avoiding obvious conflicts of interest, simultaneous service to competitors on proprietary matters, or adherence to professional society ethics. It permeates every decision and action. It means that a client willing to generate billable hours will sometimes be told to spend his money elsewhere. And it may mean great personal sacrifice to serve a client today rather than next week. From time to time it will also mean running the risk of losing a client who must be told the hard facts.

An accountant selected a computer and software package and negotiated the lease for her client. She received a fee for doing so. Several weeks following installation and training, the vendor sent the accountant a letter of appreciation and a check for $500. She could have deposited the check; it is likely that no one would ever have known. Or she could have returned the check to the manufacturer. Instead, she had the good sense to endorse the check over to her client and deliver it, indicating that the client had obviously been overcharged by $500. The good will and favorable word of mouth that followed was worth far more than $500. Placing client interest ahead of any other interest is not only the right policy, but one that is often rewarded in unexpected ways.

4. An ability to generate rapport before attempting to sell. Successful professionals invest time and energy in building a meaningful relationship with prospects prior to marketing and selling them, for the best clients are those with whom a significant and genuine relationship has been established. Creating such relationships is time-consuming but very rewarding. Today, given a choice, people do business with those who they believe have their sincere interest and well-being at heart. They don't want to be sold; they want to be helped. Consultants unable to communicate that their services are motivated by a desire to aid the client will either fail or be far less successful than they could be.

5. A dedication to developing a marketing strategy based on creating image and reputation. Those in need of professional services are far more likely to retain consultants they regard as knowledgeable, resourceful authorities than those they look upon merely as salespeople. Successful business development mandates that the consultant concentrate marketing efforts on building and communicating an image of being one who advances the state of the art and communicates about such advances. Being perceived as state-of-the-art, cutting-edge, respected, informed, sought-after, and even well connected should be the foundation of any marketing plan. The most successful have worked hard to establish a reputation as the leading authority within their niche market or specialty.

6. An ability to market results, not technology. Many professionals limit their success because they fail to sell results and benefits and instead concentrate on selling technology. They hide behind jargon and technical approach. However, clients rarely care about what's inside the "black box"; they buy results and benefits. Thus, the successful consultant develops the art of communicating with the client in those terms.

It is much like a dining experience in a five-star restaurant. As a patron, you expect to be served a fine meal with decorum and taste. The frantic conditions in the kitchen are not your concern, nor should they be.

The professional unable to translate technology into tangible benefits will limit the growth of his or her practice. The more tangible a professional can make his or her services, the easier it will be for the prospective client to see the benefits of making use of those services.

7. A commitment to avoid creating an impression that one is hungry and needy.   No one wishes to do business with someone perceived to be needy, hungry, or unsuccessful. The most successful professionals avoid any appearance of needing the business. Obviously, clients and others recognize that the professional needs clients to stay in business, but they will be far less inclined to do business with someone they feel is in need of their business.

The consultant needs to appear more like a busy surgeon than a desperate used-car dealer. Being too available, too bending, too negotiable, too flexible is never in the consultant's interest. Despite this, the professional must not be perceived as uncooperative and uninterested. A subtle balance must be struck. The prospective client should come to recognize that he needs the professional more than the professional needs the client. Accordingly, the consultant must establish policies for doing business that are appropriate for his or her practice and insist that those served adhere to those policies. Obviously, such policies must be reasonable and acceptable.

8. An ability to create the impression of accessibility and helpfulness.   Those who feel that they may have a need for professional or consulting services are often unwilling to contact a consultant because of two fears. First, they fear that they will be perceived as uninformed, inexperienced, or incapable. Second, they are concerned that they will become obligated for (high) fees prior to determining whether they need professional assistance in general or upon retaining the services of the consultant contacted. Marketing success requires that the consultant always be perceived as open, helpful, nonthreatening, accessible, and willing to discuss the benefits of retaining his services. Although it is not required that the professional avoid being compensated during the needs analysis stage, it is often helpful to business development. In any case, it is always important that the prospective client be informed of the nature of the financial obligation that will be incurred.

A plastic surgeon found that much valuable time was being wasted with initial consultations that resulted in the patient's decision not to retain his services. So he established a policy of charging for the initial consultation. When they sought appointments, patients were informed of the policy. Approximately 18 percent elected not to make an appointment. The policy not only compensated the plastic surgeon for his time, but also served as a screening device to deter the less serious.

9. A recognition of the important distinction between marketing and selling.   Consultants must engage in both marketing and selling to build viable practices. Success requires that the professional understand the difference between these two promotional activities. Marketing involves all activities that are designed to establish the image and reputation of the consultant and to make the market aware of the availability of his or her services. The opportunity to sell results from successful marketing and involves all activities that cause an interested prospect to engage the services of the consultant. Some professionals feel that they need do only one or the other, or they cannot see the fine distinction between the two. Both are vital. And the ability to know when one is engaged in marketing, as opposed to selling, is crucial.

Marketing makes the task of selling easier; it sets expectations, it informs, it educates. Consider the speed with which the modern shopper wheels through a 35,000-square-foot supermarket. In 15 or 20 minutes the shopper arrives at the check-out counter with a hundred dollars worth of products piled high in a shopping cart. Such speed of decision making and self-service has been made possible by marketing. Imagine how much slower and more expensive the shopping process would be if the proprietor of the general store still had to personally convince (sell) us on each product.

While this is obvious with respect to products, many professionals miss the significance of this analogy for their own practices.

The better they can inform the market of the value of their services, the needs they can solve, and the results they will produce for a client, the easier the selling job they will experience. Client awareness of and appreciation for the image and reputation of a particular consultant can be created through either indirect, public-relations-type marketing activities or direct marketing strategies, or both. But even the best and most effective marketing does not eliminate the need for selling, for selling involves the art of demonstrating to an interested and informed client the wisdom of engaging the professional's services and allows the professional the opportunity to customize and particularize in relation to the prospect's specific needs.

10. An adherence to the principles of test marketing. Even the most successful marketers make mistakes, and because they are creative and innovative, they tend to make the biggest mistakes. Marketing is an art, not a science. Successful private practice professionals know this and test the effectiveness and efficiency of every marketing strategy. They are careful not to take their own ideas too seriously. Far too many consultants get an idea and invest either abundant time or dollars, or both, without testing to find out if their creativity will be well received in the market. Testing requires discipline and time. Those professionals who avoid marketing until they need the business have a tendency to rush their marketing. They look for the big hit, quickly, and they elect not to test because they feel they don't have time to do so. But this is usually costly. One marketing consultant finds it necessary to remind his clients constantly of the importance of testing by saying, "You have been poor for so long anyway, can't you wait just one more month to become wealthy, and take the time to test your idea?"

11. A discipline that allows one to bury his or her ego. Professionals, like everyone else, love to be recognized and honored for their achievements. However, success often requires that the professional avoid the limelight and allow others—the client and the client's staff—to obtain recognition for successes. But this is difficult and requires discipline, for professionals tend to be more egocentric than others; high educational attainment and a long track record of successes often contribute to their egocentricity. They also are often viewed as a threat to the careers and objectives of those with whom they work. In taking credit for results and accomplishments, professionals can elevate this threat to such a degree that it has the potential to hurt client satisfaction, future business, and referrals. Developing the art of humility and fine-tuning the skill of sharing credit while still making sure that those who are important know of the professional's contributions are important for building a successful practice.

12. A devotion to the value of referral marketing. In most cases, a successful professional can, in relatively short order, develop a practice in which more than 80 percent of all business comes from referrals. There is no more cost-efficient or effective business development strategy than referral marketing. But, to be effective, referral marketing must be sophisticated and strategic. Assiduous attention to the objectives and proven-effective methods of referral marketing are really the lifeblood of the most successful professional practices.

13. A commitment to the consistency and regularity of marketing. It has often been said that the best time to borrow money is when you don't need it. If this is true for getting credit, it is even more true for marketing professional services. The time to market is not when one does not have business and is desperate, needy, and hungry. To be effective, marketing must be constant and ongoing. Successful consultants must treat marketing with the same dedication that they treat their most valued clients. A regular, consistent, continuing schedule of marketing activities must be planned and implemented. Nothing, not even client responsibilities, can be allowed to interfere. For without marketing there will be no practice worth speaking of and no future clients.

Many professionals attempt to avoid marketing, preferring to spend their time doing the work that marketing makes possible. The press of client obligations becomes, for them, the best excuse for not marketing. Nothing is more damaging to building a successful practice. The professional must limit the amount of time expended on client work and charge a sufficiently high fee to ensure that consistent and meaningful marketing is an integral part of practice management.

As you study the marketing and selling strategies that follow, keep these principles of successful professional practice in mind. If necessary, come back and review them. The proper selection of strategies, based on solid principles and philosophies of practice development and implemented with creativity and taste, will benefit you handsomely—economically, professionally, and personally.

2

INDIRECT MARKETING:
Building an Image and
Reputation That Encourages
Prospects to Seek You Out

Professionals traditionally have ignored the importance of marketing in building a successful practice. Some regard marketing as beneath their dignity, as something best relegated to salespeople. Others simply do not know how to go about marketing their services, relying instead on their technical expertise to make them successful. More often than not, they do a better job of delivering services than they do of selling those services in the first place.

However, marketing professional and consulting services is essential. To obtain more and better clients, increase profitability, and enhance overall practice success, professionals must accept the importance of marketing and must develop and implement a marketing strategy or plan that incorporates proven, effective promotional strategies.

Building a professional image or reputation is the vital foundation for the successful marketing of consulting services. Once you have built and enhanced your professional image and stature, you are able to make use of other marketing techniques that will make you even more effective in the marketplace.

The proven marketing formula is a very simple one. It is always in your interest to have prospective clients seek you out rather than for you to solicit their business. If the prospects do not seek you out because they are too shy or too embarrassed or don't know how to, it will be to your advantage for them to know who you are when you do make the initial contact. In addition, you should always provide services on your terms, not someone else's.

There are various strategies that will enhance your professional stature and reputation, gain you exposure, and indirectly promote the services you provide—causing potential clients to seek you out and retain your services. These strategies include, but are by no means limited to, the following:

1. Networking.   Any good marketing plan begins with networking—the art of making and using contacts. However, networking is truly beneficial only when you actively pursue it instead of being a passive member of the networking crowd. You will meet contacts and prospects for your services through your marketing efforts, business dealings, and social life. It is to your benefit to keep in touch with these potential clients and referral sources—phone to say hello, clip and send articles of interest to them, keep them posted on what's new in your life. This is effective networking, serving to make you—and keep you—known to people who might benefit from your services and/or might refer clients.

2. Being listed in directories.   The first place many look for professional help is in the yellow pages of the local telephone directory or in professional directories. While being listed may not enhance your reputation, it will make you more accessible. It enables those who learn about you to contact you.

3. Attending professional and trade association meetings. Merely attending association meetings is not an effective promotional strategy; however, being active and vocal in the group, positioning yourself as a leader, will make you more prominent in your area of specialty and more visible to potential clients.

4. Making speeches and presentations. Offering your services as a speaker to groups (such as trade and professional associations, civic groups, corporations) that would be likely to have prospects for your services as members (employees) can increase your visibility, enhance your reputation as an authority, and gain you clients.

5. Conducting seminars. Developing and/or conducting seminars of interest to your potential clients can gain you exposure to those who would benefit from your services and can be an additional source of income as well.

6. Writing articles and/or letters to the editor. When your articles, surveys, letters, etc., are published in newspapers, magazines, and trade and professional journals, potential clients and referral sources will notice that your ideas and information are of sufficient value to be communicated by the press. The more frequently your name and ideas are seen in print, the more you will establish yourself as an authority in your field, as someone with valuable insight to offer.

7. Writing and publishing a newsletter. This strategy has several far-reaching benefits: It allows you to communicate with clients, prospects, colleagues, and others on a regular basis; enhances your professional image and credibility as an authority; gains you exposure to more prospects for your professional services; and can provide an additional source of income.

8. Developing and marketing information products. Creating and selling information products—such as books, manuals, software, audio and video tapes, databases, etc.—is an excellent way of indirectly promoting yourself and the services you provide. It familiarizes prospects with your expertise and the various services you provide, and allows those unable to afford your professional services (at this time) to benefit from your knowledge and experience. Moreover, it provides a source of passive and accrual income, freeing you, at least in part, from a dependency on clock-hour income.

It isn't necessary to use all of these strategies; perhaps only two or three are appropriate for you, your profession, and the services you provide, and two or three are probably all that you'll have time for. For example, if you don't enjoy standing in front of groups and giving lectures, by all means avoid making speeches and presentations; if you adopt any strategies with which you are uncomfortable, you will most likely be unsuccessful using them and they will not enhance your reputation and promote your services.

So, select and employ the indirect marketing strategies that you find comfortable, effective, and appropriate. Through them, you will gain exposure to the best prospects for your services and foster your reputation as an authority in the field. Thus, you build a professional image that serves as the foundation for other marketing techniques, enabling you to promote your services most effectively and produce more and better business down the road.

Q1

If I am really one of the best professionals in my field, do I need to market my services?

Professionals who rely exclusively on their reputations and/or competence to gain business assume that if they simply take care of their reputations, their reputations will take care of them. This is partially true in that a poor reputation can undermine all your other efforts to grow. However, while a good reputation provides the foundation for a successful practice, it is only a foundation, not an active marketing plan for gaining new clients and business. Moreover, a reputation does not take care of itself; you must take care of it because:

1. Your reputation often goes out of date, giving you a high rating on abilities that no one needs anymore.
2. Your reputation spreads haphazardly, and it probably does not reach all of the prospective clients you want to reach.

3. Your reputation may become distorted through word of mouth. You may not be credited with the kind of expertise that best suits your marketing approach and the services you provide.

4. The passive approach does not bring those first few clients in the door or allow the established practitioner to attract and acquire the most desirable clients and contracts.

Despite the pitfalls of relying on reputation to bring you business, all too many professionals fall for "the Harvard–M.I.T. Fallacy"—the belief that, "Since my services are obviously superior to anything else available, I can just sit here and the world will beat a path to my door."

Dozens of professionals who have been graduated from prestigious universities and who are technical masters have adopted this attitude and have ignored the necessity of marketing, even when faced with financial failure. They refused to believe that anyone could be a member of their elite group and still have to do anything as vulgar as compete for business in the hurly-burly of the marketplace.

Some, in fact, succeed very nicely. They are so brilliant or creative that word-of-mouth reports of their excellence spread so fast that they are overbooked two months after hanging out their shingle. But most are not this lucky.

They hide behind professionalism as an excuse for not marketing. Fifty years ago, when the competitive restraint of the "encumbered" professions had a colorable pretense of being in the public interest, such logic may have made sense. But with recent Supreme Court and FTC rulings that these restraints are contrary to the public interest, the tide has turned. Today, it is absolutely legitimate to compete for professional business, and only a very small fraction of potential clients consider active (but tasteful) marketing inappropriate.

But the best confirmation that the Harvard–M.I.T. Fallacy is a fallacy is the number of professionals who suffer from it. Most of them are technically excellent, but certainly not overwhelmed with work (or even modestly busy).

Properly done, marketing can be both tasteful and productive.

Q2

Which is more important for success, marketing or technical competence?

No single factor is more vital to success in professional practice than marketing your services. Technical competence is necessary but not sufficient. Despite the paramount importance of careful, creative, and consistent marketing, most consultants are less than skillful when it comes to promoting themselves and their services.

Three major factors contribute to such an inability and uncertainty with marketing: (1) Professionals tend to be technically oriented, not marketing oriented. They prefer to expend time and energy on identifying, diagnosing, and solving client problems, and they find such activity far more rewarding and meaningful than promoting, marketing, and selling. (2) Professionals tend to look down on marketing as an activity unworthy of their valuable time and effort; many feel that if they are good at what they do, there should be little need for marketing. They believe that the world will beat a path to their door, but, unfortunately, it is necessary at the least to clear the brush from the path if you expect anyone to find the door. (3) Professionals are not trained or schooled in marketing. Even marketing consultants often lack knowledge and experience appropriate to marketing professional practices in particular.

Research on more than 10,000 professional practices clearly demonstrates that creative marketing is the determining factor in the success of a practice. While technical competence will certainly magnify the results of marketing and self-promotion, it is not a substitute.

Yes, marketing is absolutely essential to your success as a consultant and if you—like many professionals—feel uncertain about your abilities as a marketer, now is the time to commit to learning and using the marketing tools and techniques vital to building a successful practice.

Q3

How much of my time should be devoted to marketing?

The key to a successful practice lies in careful, creative, and consistent marketing of yourself and your services. Devote about 15 to

25 percent of your working hours—each and every week—to marketing and selling. The time to market is not when you have run out of clients or backlog, but before.

Moreover, spend a minimum of 50 percent of your marketing time on activities that will build your image and reputation as a knowledgeable resource in your field of expertise. Time spent giving speeches, writing articles, contributing meaningfully to professional and trade organizations, publishing your own newsletter, etc., is the most productive marketing you can do.

The balance of your marketing time should be spent developing the business of specific clients. Such efforts may include pursuing quality leads, holding initial exploratory meetings, proposing solution concepts, writing proposals, following up, and closing business.

Many professionals find it difficult to switch back and forth between marketing and delivering services. Most would prefer to expend their time fulfilling rather than generating new business. Don't allow a heavy client workload or a preference for working on client assignments to become an excuse for avoiding marketing. Treat marketing as equal in importance to your most significant client. If you really are too busy to devote 15 to 25 percent of your time to marketing, you should think about reducing time spent on providing services. How? The four most frequently employed strategies are hiring associates, subcontracting to other independent professionals, turning away less profitable assignments, and increasing fees (to maintain income while working fewer hours).

Q4
What marketing strategies are used by the most successful consultants and professionals?

Research demonstrates that indirect, public-relations-type marketing strategies are more widely used by the highest-income professionals.*

The Professional Consultant and Information Marketing Report (May 1989), copyright Howard L. Shenson, CMC, 20750 Ventura Boulevard, Woodland Hills, CA 91364.

Marketing Strategies Used by Professionals
Percentage of Respondents Using Identified Marketing Strategy
(Income Equals Personal Pre-Tax Income after Business Expenses)

Marketing Strategy	All Professionals	Professionals with Annual Pre-tax Income Greater than $100,000	Professionals with Annual Pre-tax Income Less than $50,000
Cold personal calls	52.6	14.4	73.7
Direct mail brochures/ Sales letter to cold lists	62.3	18.7	69.2
Provision of no-charge diagnostic services to pre-qualified leads	39.7	19.6	55.4
Promotion to similar clients on basis of referrals or names obtained from clients	55.6	69.6	22.4
Lectures to civic, trade, and professional audiences	20.7	39.4	9.4
Writing articles, books, newsletters for trade, professional, and civic audiences	18.3	37.8	6.3

Q5
What are the prime reasons consulting practices fail?

The media constantly point out the risks of small business owner-ship. Some studies suggest that as many as 50 percent of new busi-nesses fail within the first three years. More conservative studies suggest the number to be more like 25 to 33⅓ percent. What about professional practices? They are less likely to fail and when they do it is often for different reasons. The explanation for most small busi-

The majority of lower-income professionals report that direct marketing strategies are not very effective in producing business. Why do professionals continue to pursue such direct selling strategies even after they have proven unsatisfactory? Many are simply not aware of alternative strategies they could pursue to market their services effectively.

It is to your best advantage to research and develop indirect marketing strategies, such as those mentioned, that will have the most profitable impact on your financial and professional success.

ness failures is either undercapitalization or poor management. The smaller professional practice is often (relatively) immune to these factors. Management of a one- or two-person practice isn't too complex, and with the use of proper, proven-effective marketing strategies, the capital requirements should be modest.

The principal reasons a professional practice fails can best be explained by the following factors:

1. **Inability of some professionals to function successfully on their own.** Some professionals need to work in an environment that is augmented by support staff, collegial peers, and disciplined supervision.

2. **Unwillingness or inability to market.** Some professionals are unwilling to market and sell their services.

3. **Failure to focus on target markets.** Clients result from tailored, specific marketing. Some professionals who are not successful are unable to translate their skills into specific services that the market wants to buy.

4. **Failure to market with consistency and regularity.** Those who are unsuccessful frequently fail to maintain ongoing marketing momentum. They market only when they have run out of clients.

5. **High overhead or fiscal imprudence.** Good fortune often produces a mind-set that billings will remain consistently at a

high level. This causes the professional to commit to too high a level of overhead or to take too much from current revenues for personal expenses.

6. **Unwillingness to be frank, honest, or direct with clients.** This can lead to a reputation that the professional's services are expendable and it reduces the motivation to refer.

7. **Inability or unwillingness to communicate in terms relevant to the client.** Some professionals intentionally communicate with technical jargon because they believe it will be impressive to the prospect or client. Others do so because they are truly unable to communicate their expertise in conventional terms.

8. **Failure to expand at an appropriate rate and at the right time.** The press of client work becomes so burdensome that there is insufficient time to manage the practice or maintain an appropriate level of marketing activity.

> Discipline yourself to take an amount equal to 10 percent of your daily bank deposit and place it in a savings account. Do this daily. Pretend that the money doesn't exist, and never permit yourself to tap it. When you retire, you will have a sizeable retirement fund, and in the event of a real business emergency you will have funds to call upon.

Q6
What are the early warning signs that my practice may be in trouble?

Be watchful for the following five early signals that suggest a consulting practice might be in trouble. If such signals are caught early enough, you can take action to ensure long-term viability.

   1. Inability to pay your bills on a timely basis. Often the result of inability or failure to collect from clients, this is a primary factor in the demise of otherwise healthy practices. Take steps now to ensure that sloppy credit practices and lazy collection procedures don't sink you.

2. Downward trend in gross billings/sales. Ups and downs are common, but look at the longer trends over 6 to 18 months. Be sure that you are keeping pace with technological and market changes. Services (and products) that satisfied your clients in the past may not be right for today—at least for the same class of clientele at fee levels they have been willing to pay.

3. Slowly rising overhead. As your practice or business matures, it is common to demand or expect more amenities. Rising overhead is not itself a problem if it is supported by increased billings. Measure overhead regularly as a percentage of gross billings or sales to ensure that rising costs are keeping pace with business growth. Keep expenses variable, and consider paying cash for equipment or leasehold improvements to keep the monthly nut manageable.

4. Creative burnout. Find a reliable way to measure your motivation and interest in your business, your work, and your clients. Client demand will fall if you fail to remain intense, motivated, and state-of-the-art. Protect the future of your business by scheduling time for formal and informal professional renewal, brainstorming, and research. Take time to watch market and social trends. Don't schedule such a heavy workload that you are forced to be creative when you can't be.

Having a mission will reduce the prospect of burnout. If you are asking yourself, "Is that all there is?" you may already be suffering from the early stages of burnout. Successful professionals set goals and quests for themselves and pursue them. Missions provide purpose to the daily routine. Your mission is not the client's. Have vision; discover what you want to accomplish and achieve for yourself, and pursue it.

5. Chasing undesirable business. Look for signs that clients are taxing or constant management headaches. Avoid clients who really can't afford you or who fail to benefit from doing business with you. Raise your sights and concentrate on the better heeled, more appreciative clients.

Also: Avoid emotional involvement with clients. Watch for early signs that they may be in trouble. Take steps to protect yourself and/or extricate yourself from the relationship before they sink you!

> There is more to a successful practice than marketing your services, gaining clients, and providing services. Yes, these are the foundations of your business—they are what you do; however, periodically take time to assess the warning signs that your practice may be in trouble, above, so that you can catch problem areas in time to keep your practice healthy, profitable, and thriving.

Q7
How greatly will the name I select for my practice affect my chances for success?

Your name is important, but usually not central, to the success of your practice. Most professionals select one of three types of names:

- One that identifies them personally.
- One that describes the nature of the services provided.
- One that suggests an institutional and perhaps not-for-profit orientation such as "institute," "center," or "foundation."

There are advantages and disadvantages to each. Care should be taken to consider each prospective name in light of these advantages and disadvantages.

Using Your Name as the Name, or Part of the Name, of the Practice

Examples:
Cynthia Jones, CFP
Robert T. Johnson & Associates

People in our society are strongly attracted to personalities. Personal identification seems to be important in an age of impersonal organizations and bureaucratic complexity. Rock stars, actors, and athletes, of course, all seem to capitalize on this trend. Professional practitioners can too.

Yet there are several reasons you might not wish to use your name as your company name:

1. If you are incorporated, using your name to insulate your assets from liability that results from business decisions sometimes provides less protection when the consumer reasonably may be confused by a lack of clear distinction between the individual and the business.

2. Should you ever declare business bankruptcy, it would be wise if your personal name did not have to appear in the public records. It might confuse people and the resulting personal publicity might not be in your interest.

3. If you elect to sell your corporation or your name, it might not be in your interest to do so if you don't want your name associated with the buyer.

These factors, of course, all relate to the business when it is a corporation. Even if you don't plan to incorporate, you may later elect to do so. This might be done after your business name has been established and is well-known. A change in name at that time might be more difficult than the initial selection of a name when you are starting your practice.

The laws in almost all jurisdictions require that if you are doing business under a name other than your own legal name (or your corporate legal name), certain procedures of notification or registration are required to identify the individuals who own the business and protect the public. This applies to any alteration of your name, even the mere addition of the words "and Associates" to your personal name. The procedure is easy, usually involving nominal expense.

Using a Name That Describes the Services You Provide

> *Examples:*
> Creative Advertising Services
> Environmental Reporting Associates
> The Bankruptcy Law Group

Such names instantly communicate to prospects the services you provide and can assist clients in locating you. However, they lack the "personal" identification associated with using your own name, and they may be so specific that they limit future marketing effectiveness as technology changes and/or services provided expand. You wouldn't want to have to make a name change later that would result in a handle like:

> Duke's Buggy Whip & Muffler Repair
> or
> The Center for Time & Motion Study/Human Potential Development

Yet a name that provides too general and vague a description of the services you provide lacks specific relevance, for example:

> Pacific Management Consultants

Management consultants provide a wide variety of services. The prospect has no idea whether Pacific is a boutique specializing in establishing quality circles in financial institutions or a full-line management consulting firm purporting to handle just about anything.

Using an Institutional or Nonprofit Sounding Name

Examples:
The Center for Policy Studies
National Endowment for Financial Options
The Institute for Personal Studies

Such names were much more popular a number of years ago, when there was greater distrust of business and an aversion to profit. While they are still used to some extent, the popularity of business and entrepreneurship and the greater acceptance of the notion that the business of business is to make profit have made this type of name less popular today. But remember: Social and political trends change, and at some future point "profit" may be less highly regarded. Many professionals doing business with government or nonprofits found this kind of name to have a strong marketing advantage. It made them appear, or so they thought, more like their clients.

Other things being equal, it is often best to select a name that includes your name or is simply your name. In professional practice, you are the product, and every time your name is used, you are promoting the product you sell—your professional services. If you stop to think about it, the vast majority of all the largest professional and consulting practices contain the name of one or more individuals, usually the founder(s). This does not mean, however, that you should necessarily change the name of your practice. In most cases, the name used is not that crucial.

Regardless of what the actual name of your firm is, you may want to protect it. The protection of a name is a very complex matter and you would be well advised to obtain the assistance of legal authority. In many states, for example, a corporation wishing to prevent others from using its corporate name is assisted in doing so. All corporations are required to register their name, and if the name is already in use, the corporations commissioner will not allow the name to be used by a new corporation. Large companies usually seek to register their name in all states in which they expect to do business in the future. Doing so is both costly and time consuming for a small firm. Increasingly, professionals are taking the steps necessary to have their name meet the criteria for a registered trade name. A patent and copyright attorney may be helpful to you in this regard.

Q8
What information should be included on my business card?

Avoid using your business card as an advertising billboard. Don't list the 29 different services you provide to your clients; it makes you look like a jack-of-all-trades. The less said the better. Descriptions of services provided have a tendency to reduce the number of people who will have an interest in contacting you. If people ask for your business card, they most likely already know what you do. And if you give your very plain, simple, and sophisticated business card to people who don't know what you do, they may call or write to find out—on the chance that you might provide services that they need.

On the subject of business cards, not everyone you encounter will have a business card, and you will meet some who have already given away their in-pocket supply. However, it is in your interest to have these individuals' names in your files, in your database, or on your mailing list. Carry a supply of "request for information" cards, which could be postcards with your address and phone on one side and a place for the user to provide their name, title, firm, address, phone number, and other information on the

---

Avoid the temptation to look at every business card received, or consider every contact made, a source of referrals. Be selective. There is only so much time available for marketing and business development; expend that time in the most productive fashion. On the other hand, don't be too quick to dismiss potential sources for future business without suggesting to them how you might be of service and giving them a chance to demonstrate the ways in which they might benefit you.

reverse. When someone desires technical or professional information that you could provide or more information about your services, simply say something like "Please fill out this card or, if you prefer, give me your business card and I will see that this information is mailed to you first thing tomorrow."

Q9
Should I use a résumé to promote my services?

Never use a résumé to promote your services. Many professionals sense the need to have some type of written communication to hand to or mail to a prospect. Résumés are so commonplace that they tend to be filed away and forgotten without ever being read. More important—almost all résumés fail to be organized in such a fashion as to communicate the critical data the professional wants the prospective client to consider. You may have to develop a résumé to satisfy the files of an existing client, but it is a disastrous first marketing piece.

A piece of paper to help market your services may not be necessary at all. But in many cases having something to hand out or leave behind has value. If so, develop a specially crafted message designed to interest the prospect in your services. Ideally, the piece developed should be so specific to the prospect's needs and interests that it compels the prospect to engage your services. This can be accomplished with a well-written letter. Once written and demonstrated to be effective, such a letter can be developed into a practice brochure or capabilities statement.

Q10
Are brokers effective for securing new clients?

In recent years, professionals have been solicited by an increasing number of brokers purporting to be expert at obtaining business for them. Are brokers productive?

Brokers have proven to be most effective when assisting the professional to gain business contacts in specialized niche markets. One brokerage, now out of business, was quite successful in helping consultants and other professionals obtain expert witness work with attorneys. For the most part, however, brokers have not been a productive marketing tool. Why? Almost all prospects want to meet the professional personally. Effective marketing for professionals requires that they demonstrate their understanding of the client's need and communicate the creativity of their approach. In technical disciplines, it is often impossible for the broker to be sufficiently conversant with the subject to do the job.

Brokers tend to work in one of two ways. Some take a percentage of the billings collected by the professional; others charge an up-front fee, which can be several hundred to a few thousand dollars. The professional should be very cautious about paying any fees up front, for experience suggests that such payments are often the last productive communication between the parties. How much do those who work on a percentage-of-billings basis charge? Most charge from about 12 to 35 percent, averaging about 17 percent. The range is best explained by the amount of activity the broker expends on behalf of the professional. Some do little more than maintain a résumé in their files and, upon receipt of a request for services from a client, mail out a résumé. Others expend considerable marketing effort.

But effort does not mean success! Discussions with numerous professionals represented by brokers suggest that the business produced is far less than the professionals expected. The initial decision to engage the services of a broker is often viewed as a solution to all marketing problems. In quick order, however, the professional soon realizes that the broker will supply only a little extra business—if that.

It is far better for most consultants to expend time and energy (and even dollars) improving their own marketing and selling skills.

If you do make use of a broker, the broker should have a strict philosophy of ensuring that the client is aware of the relationship. The fact that the broker profits from promoting your services obviously influences the broker's recommendations to the client. This is a prejudice the client should be informed of. And it would be clearly unethical for the broker to double dip—to charge the client a fee for finding a qualified professional while also charging the professional a fee for being found.

Q11
Should I promote my consulting services to corporate personnel departments?

In almost all cases, it is to your advantage to stay away from personnel departments (unless you are an advisor or consultant to personnel departments). Consultants engaged by operating management to work for the corporation hinder the growth and empire building of the personnel department. You do not want to wind up in the résumé files of personnel departments. When selling to corporations, you must reach key decision-makers in operating departments. The people with line decision-making authority are the ones able and motivated to commit for your services. How do you find the key decision-makers? Research. Talk to managers, secretaries, competitors; they know who makes the decisions.

In many corporations, the decision to engage your services may be a joint decision. The personnel department may play an advisory role; the line decision-makers may discuss use of your services with personnel before contracting with you. Thus, while it is not in your interest to expend much time and effort marketing the personnel department, it may be useful for you to make them aware of your capabilities. Develop a positive image, keep personnel informed, try to get the personnel department staff to see you as a resource and not a threat.

Q12
Should I ever recommend other consultants or professionals to potential clients? Does it ever pay to promote my competitors?

Expend energy promoting your competition for referrals and subcontract or joint assignments. In many fields, 11 to 21 percent of all new business comes from the competition. Recognize that your colleagues may have assignments outside their field of precise specialty, business that they are too busy to handle, or projects of such scope that they will need to retain the services of another professional to work jointly.

When you are involved in a subcontract or joint assignment

with another professional (or competitor), avoid all activities that might be viewed by the other professional or the client as an attempt to market yourself directly for future business. If the client perceives that working directly with you or referring your services to others would be desirable, they are well aware of the possibility of contacting you in this regard. But marketing the client directly is certainly inappropriate and will greatly hurt future business that might emanate from your peers.

If you are having difficulty finding enough time to do adequate marketing and image building while still serving clients in a timely, professional fashion, you probably need to expand your capability of delivering services by hiring a professional employee or setting up subcontractor relationships that give you access to others who can help you serve clients.

When working with subcontractors and associates, be sure to have a written agreement that details the terms of the work and includes a noncompete clause, protecting you from their setting up business on their own and taking your clients with them.

Q13
Can responding to help-wanted ads produce consulting business?

On the surface, it seems logical. Scores of ads appear each week— available for the price of a newspaper—purporting to need the very services you offer. And since the ads are repeated over and over again, shouldn't these advertisers be willing to obtain the necessary talents and skills from an outside professional? However, experience strongly suggests that responding to the help-wanted ads is most often a poor use of your very valuable time. Organizations seeking full-time employees normally want just that. Newspaper ads usually bring you in contact with the personnel department, and personnel departments tend to have an aversion to making use of independent professionals, perhaps because they may consider being unable to find full-time employees at reasonable cost to be a negative reflection on the job they are doing.

On the other hand, selectively answering the right ad at the right time can be beneficial. Consider these two success stories. In the first one, the professional is a highly paid technical consultant providing services in a field where few full-time personnel are available. The second is a person working in aerospace. The first has secured clients through help-wanted advertising but usually finds the terms and conditions of the engagement somewhat unacceptable. The clients frequently are somewhat unwilling to pay his expected fee, and they seek too long-term an assignment on his part. In addition, they often want him to devote more hours per month than he finds appropriate. The second professional believes he has been successful because of the great shortage of available personnel in his field. Thus, such a marketing tactic might be worth a try if you feel that your specialty is in short supply, particularly if you provide a technical service that is in great demand. But if you are really needed and in demand, other marketing strategies may be more effective and result in getting business on terms more acceptable to you.

Q14
Does it pay for my professional firm to be listed in directories?

Many in need of your services do not know how to find someone with your expertise and will try both telephone and professional directories. Facilitate connections by being listed in directories. Be listed in the yellow pages of the major telephone directory in your market area. An expensive, large, and flashy ad isn't necessary and could be regarded as unprofessional and, thus, counterproductive. But a listing or small ad spelling out your services should, if properly written, produce a number of potential leads.

Even more importantly, be listed in all trade and professional directories that reach your target markets. More than half of all associations will allow you to be listed free of charge, as it is a service to their members. Use *The Encyclopedia of Associations* (Gale Research Co., Book Tower, Detroit, Michigan 48226) or other guides to identify the associations related to your market; then simply inquire about the nature and availability of their directory listings. It may be appropriate for you to be listed in any directory covering your profession. For example, many professionals would find it advisable to be listed in the best-known and most comprehensive directory of consultants: Gale Research Company's *Consult-*

ants and Consulting Organizations Directory. There is no charge to be listed in the directory, which can be found in major public, academic, and corporate libraries. It includes the professional's name, address, and telephone number, as well as a description of the services provided. The reader is able to locate desired professionals through both field of specialization and geographic indexes.

You probably won't be able to retire as a result of being listed in a few directories, but the decision to invest a day's time to ensure that you are listed in 15 to 20 directories pertinent to your specialty will no doubt pay for itself several times over.

Q15
Is networking really a profitable use of my time?

If you network the way most consultants do, probably not. Marketing authorities have been pushing networking so much that their advice may be falling on deaf ears. But you can make the time spent networking exceedingly profitable. Most believe that networking is good, of course, but with so many people networking these days, the early successes enjoyed by networkers are not currently being experienced as much. You need to be more creative. Just standing around with a cup of coffee or a cocktail in your hand is not very effective anymore.

Most networking is based on being just one of the crowd—a form of subtle, "sneak-up-on-ya" marketing. Don't waste time being just one of the crowd. It may have worked when you were the only one networking, but with everyone in the ballgame you need to be distinctive. Be the leader of the network. Position yourself in networking to be the one whom everyone would like to be if they could.

Join one or two professional, civic, or trade associations comprising your prospective clients and referral sources. Do so only if you are willing to become active, noticed, and powerful in the association. To be noticed and seen as a resource, work your way up the power structure and contribute generously. Avoid wasting valuable time by being simply an invisible member of many organizations.

Figure out from whom your business comes and from whom

your business should come, and develop your own network, making yourself the leader.

One professional established her own network and positioned herself as its focal point. She identified where her business was coming from and the type of clients with whom she wanted to do business. Then she organized a group that met monthly over breakfast. She appointed herself executive director of the group. Each member paid for his or her own breakfast plus a small amount to defray communication expenses. The professional coordinated, organized, led, and managed the network. Even when guest speakers were brought in, she was clever enough to require them to adjust to a format in which she interviewed them, asking pertinent questions and challenging their responses. The result? She came to be viewed by those in the network as a creative, provocative, organized professional. As you can well imagine, this was exceedingly productive for developing her practice with members of the network and many others who came to learn about her by word of mouth. That's creative networking!

After meeting someone at a mixer, meeting, or other business situation, promptly send a personal letter or note that expresses your pleasure in having met him or her and communicates that the meeting was sufficiently meaningful to you that you remember some aspect of your conversation. Avoid the appearance of a form letter that is just another "nice to have met you" communication—speak to them personally and specifically.

Q16
Will contacting past friends and associates produce significant business?

Keep in contact with people out of your past; old friends, colleagues, and classmates can be excellent sources of referrals and often turn into clients themselves. We all know people with whom we have not communicated in months or years, but this does not mean that we shouldn't start communicating now.

Unless specifically requested or encouraged to do so, the first communication (and perhaps the second and third) following the meeting of a new business or referral source should not be a solicitation to provide you with business or professional advantage. The best and most meaningful referrals come from first having established a professional relationship. Don't jump on potential opportunity too fast; you could hurt your future opportunities.

Make a list of at least two or three people from each of the following groups:

- o Neighborhood friends from childhood.
- o Classmates (elementary, junior high, high school, and college).
- o Past teachers and professors.
- o Former employers, co-workers, subordinates.
- o Past business contacts—vendors, competitors, financial contacts, etc.
- o Previous clients and prospects.
- o Past contacts from charitable, social service, and purely social relationships.
- o Others from your past who are now in positions of (potential) authority, power, and influence.

Take time to write or call these people and renew contact. We are often reluctant to renew contact because of feelings about our past relationships, but people will be pleased that you made the effort to reestablish the relationship, to say hello, or to stay in touch. Because you are calling without a specific purpose, they will be much more open and relaxed; they'll ask what you've been doing, which will naturally lead to talk about your services.

In the same vein, go through your personal telephone directory or Rolodex and divide it into twelve sections—about two letters of the alphabet for every month of the year. Set aside two or three hours each month to call the people on the list (January = A and B, February = C and D, etc.) who could be a source of referrals or direct business with whom you have not spoken in the last 90 to 120 days. The purpose? Just to say hello and inquire about their well-being. Do not attempt to solicit business or referrals. If circumstances permit, casually mention an interesting project or beneficial referral received. The conversation should end without their feeling that they have been marketed. This is an excellent technique for staying in touch, in a professional and nonoffensive way, with people who are in a position to benefit you. Some will initially communicate caution, awaiting your sales pitch. When it becomes obvious that they are not going to be pitched, they will relax and open up.

You will be surprised at how much new business and how many referrals these simple (and quite enjoyable) strategies will gain you. But don't expect immediate response. Now and then, one of these contacts will say something like, "I've been meaning to call you because I want you to _____." That's rare. But your call will serve to have you resurface in their conscious minds. Over the next two or three months, they may have some business for you. Also, you are very likely to get calls from people to whom they have referred you. Not all of these calls will result in new business. But if you spend three hours a month talking to 200 people a year and wind up with 12 new clients or projects, your investment in this marketing effort will likely have been a wise decision.

Q17
How can I effectively promote my services to previous business and professional contacts?

Personal contacts, perhaps from previous employment experience, can be an important source of clients and referrals. Because they know you and your abilities, no other group (at least when you are starting your practice) represents better potential for business. Correct handling is necessary, however, if they are not to perceive you as a nuisance and if you are to achieve maximum economic benefit from these contacts.

Once you have hung out your shingle, you can expect that

they will be just a little bit wary and perhaps even jealous. You now sell a service for which they are potential clients. Sending them a brochure or capabilities statement with a standard cover letter is rarely productive; it will only serve to modify faster the established relationship.

A better approach is to take these contacts and divide them into two groups: those whom you regard as the best potential prospects for your professional services, and those who are less valuable prospects.

With your first group in mind, create a letter (in some cases a phone call may be more appropriate) that is designed to inform your colleagues or prospects that you have severed your relationship with XYZ Industries International and have established your own practice. This is valuable information in case they need to communicate. Your letter should go on to say something like:

As you know, Joe, I value greatly your insights into the prospects and problems facing the widget industry. I would very much appreciate it if you would join me as my guest for lunch later this month to discuss several issues of great importance to me at this juncture in my career:

- What do you see as the most pressing issues consultants will be asked to deal with in the widget industry during the next five years?
- How have consultants failed in serving the widget industry in the recent past?
- What trends do you see in the industry that the trade magazines are ignoring or not covering adequately?
- What individuals and companies in the industry do you regard as the most progressive, innovative, and creative?

Joe, I would really appreciate it if you could provide me with your insights. I will call your secretary on Monday, October 8 to set a day for lunch that is convenient for you.

Personal regards,

Rest assured, Joe will have lunch with you. He will not want to miss the opportunity to tell you what to do with the rest of your life. Indeed, he will probably insist on paying for lunch.

For starters, Joe will have all kinds of questions for you. Down deep, he is likely a little jealous. He too would like to be out on his own. So he will want to know how you engineered your change and the trials and tribulations thereof. Some time will be spent discussing the questions raised in your letter, but most of the discussion will concentrate on Joe's needs, Joe's problems, Joe's desires. You can make the lunch a profitable expenditure of time by delivering an onslaught of mini proposals—describing for Joe how you could handle these needs and the general approach you would take.

This technique has been used on numerous occasions with great success. The discussion of Joe's problems inevitably results in your communicating approaches to reduce his problems. And, of course, you are available for assignment. This fact will not be lost on Joe.

Schedule a minimum of ten such lunches over a 30-day period. If you don't wind up with at least two new clients, you may have another problem—consider changing your mouthwash.

The second group—your not-as-valuable, prospects—should certainly be informed of your changed status. It would be nice to take this group to lunch too, but you can't spend the rest of your life eating lunch. If possible and practicable, design a small seminar or discussion group on two or three central issues (maybe those most frequently identified by the first group) and hold a meeting that will allow you to communicate with several people simultaneously. The next regional or national trade or professional association meeting might be just the place. If that is not workable, send your new brochure along with a special, personalized letter that provides some reason for continued and regular communications.

You will, of course, modify these suggestions to be appropriate for your circumstances. But, be sure to replicate the important underlying principles. People like to talk about themselves, they like to have their advice sought, they like to give their opinions, they want to guide and direct you. And most importantly, the best

> Cultivate business and referral sources with broadcast power. Those in positions of influence or authority, such as association executives, editors, and chairpersons of conferences can magnify your opportunities significantly. Identify the people who have made significant contributions to your field of specialty and communicate with them to gain further information about their work. This helps you to develop a relationship with shakers and movers, assists you in being known and recognized, and may well lead to desirable business and/or referrals.

way of marketing your services often is to give the impression that you are not marketing at all.

Q18
How can I get an appointment with the high-level prospects that I really want to see?

Many consultants are frustrated by their inability to obtain an appointment to promote their services with the people they regard as shakers and movers. They say, "If I could only meet with Ms. X for 30 minutes, I could convince her of how valuable a resource I would be for accomplishing her objectives." But, they can't get past the palace guards. Why? Palace guards are installed to ensure that people with unnecessary and nonessential business don't waste the time of busy executives. All the tricks you have heard about for getting past secretaries, receptionists, and managers to reach the key decision-makers are really not effective. The key decision-maker will meet with you and be receptive only when you have a communication objective that is of true interest and value to him or her. The most successful professionals recognize that their success is predicated on the fact that they are viewed as being more than just another salesperson. Key decision-makers will meet with you when they view you as a resource and authority. Regardless of how professional you may view yourself, or how essential your message is, you are just another salesperson to them until you demonstrate otherwise. Thus, it is in your interest to be viewed by clients and prospects alike as someone who is advancing the state of the art, or at least communicating about the advances. And it doesn't hurt you to be perceived as well connected either.

There are many ways of accomplishing the objective—being perceived as someone other than another salesperson. Be creative in getting to see the prospects you want to see. It does not take great savvy to telephone someone and request an opportunity to see that person to sell your services. It also isn't a very successful method if the prospect isn't burning to see you. Moreover, it is often uncomfortable or inappropriate for the professional to solicit business or referrals from such individuals directly. You will be far more effective in getting to know the prospects you really desire to know, particularly when they are in positions of importance or great influence, if you can find some way of starting a relationship with them rather than just taking their time to try to sell them services they don't really think they need. Being creative might involve booking an appointment, requesting their assistance for a research or writing project you are working on, as follows:

> I would like to make an appointment to see you, Mr. Jones. I am currently conducting a study of compensation practices with HMOs (or writing an article for _____ magazine, or for your own newsletter). I understand that you have had some unique success in this area.

Rest assured, you will get the opportunity to meet Jones. Everyone likes to talk about what they've been doing and most desire publicity that could benefit their enterprise or personal career. You will learn something, and Jones will be curious about what you've learned in your other interviews. When meeting with Jones, do not solicit business or referrals; instead, use this first meeting as a basis for developing a professional relationship. The two of you now have a common interest. You have also developed a friend and contact. In the future, you can meet with him again for similar purposes and to market your services, add his name to your circulation lists and alert lists, etc. And very frequently the first meeting or subsequent meetings will result in direct business or referrals.

Make sure that your reason for contacting, meeting with, and interviewing such prospects is legitimate. If you say that you are writing an article or conducting research, you had better be doing so. And remember to send copies of the finished work to the interviewees. You can also set up additional meetings or communications to allow the people to review or modify the information, ideas, and comments you have attributed to them.

The best way to sell professional services is often not to give the impression that you are selling at all. Get to know those whom you could serve first on a professional or collegial basis and later you will be the first one they think of when they need your services or are asked to refer someone with your talents.

Q19
Do club memberships produce business?

Many professionals are able to develop excellent referrals and direct business from their social contacts. Some can turn an afternoon on the golf course or a lunch at the club into excellent future business. If you are comfortable in doing so, you should probably take advantage of the opportunity. If, however, you have difficulty doing so or feel uncomfortable in such situations, do not pursue them. Don't try to obtain business or referrals with activities that you find uncomfortable. Your lack of comfort will be obvious and your success accordingly limited.

If you want to join a country club, town club, or other social association, by all means do so. But do not join with the sole hope and intention of meeting and being seen with prominent, wealthy, influential people and thus obtaining business. It rarely happens; most people prefer to separate their business and social lives. Instead, devote effort employing proven marketing strategies with which you are relaxed, confident, and effective.

Q20
How can I make my name a household word with potential prospects or clients?

Get your name and your ideas published in the leading trade magazines and journals that your clients read on a regular basis. Comment on what important people in the field are saying; interpret general news for its impact on your clients; develop, implement, and report on surveys you conduct. Those in a position to refer or make use of your services directly will begin to notice that your thinking is of sufficient value that it is regularly picked up and communicated by the press. The more often prospects see your name and ideas in print, the more likely they will become your clients.

In addition, send letters to the editors of trade and professional publications and the daily newspaper. Communicate crisply, clearly, and intelligently a thought supporting or countering a point made in the publication; such letters should be well-written, substantiated, and somewhat controversial. The more your name and ideas are seen in print, the more you have established yourself as an authority.

Writing and publishing a monthly, bimonthly, or quarterly newsletter also increases your visibility, enhances your credibility as an authority, and lets you maintain contact with past and present friends, colleagues, clients, prospects, etc., who are all potential referral sources and/or clients. Some of the most effective letters are simply provocative philosophical thoughts word processed or typed on standard letterhead, just one to four pages long. A more sophisticated format or different length may be useful too. To be effective, your newsletter must be good and interesting. It should not be perceived as direct advertising, but the indirect promotional benefit is obvious.

Publishing your own newsletter can also let you keep prospects, former clients, and others familiar with your successes. If you want certain people to know about awards, honors, presentations, new contracts, research results, and breakthroughs but want to communicate such information unobtrusively and without boasting, publish the news in your newsletter and put these people on your circulation list. Your successes make you seem more valuable and people who know about them will be more likely to do business with you in the future.

Attending association meetings and seminars frequented by your prospective clients won't get you business unless you are visible. However, raising provocative questions, making interesting points will increase your visibility and your reputation as a knowledgeable authority. But don't monopolize time—doing so will hurt your image and incur the wrath of the presenters and the audience. A few well made points are far more effective and memorable than conducting your own seminar during someone else's presentation. During the breaks and after the presentation, circulate, making yourself visible and available to talk to; people—prospects for your services—will want to talk to you if your remarks are pertinent and insightful.

Being identified as a researcher and one who contributes to advancing the state of the art will substantively increase your reputation and exposure, thus increasing business and referrals. Devote time and effort to designing and implementing research projects that provide valuable information to those who will read the results of your efforts and help you to get your information published. Such research need not be highly sophisticated or time-consuming. Simple surveys and questionnaires that measure trends or point out directions in thinking and behavior are often sufficient and help to create recognition that you are a knowledgeable resource at the cutting edge of your area of expertise.

Q21
How can I encourage the press to publicize my services?

Encourage press coverage of your ideas and activities by identifying press contacts pertinent to your prospects and referral sources and then communicating with these contacts on a regular basis. Depending upon your market and your area of specialization, relevant press contacts may be reasonably broad or narrow and may represent general interest or highly specialized publications.

Read the publications produced by your press contacts, noting items with which you agree and disagree, and write letters to the editor in response. Send copies or summaries of your speeches; many journalists find them more important or timely than an article. Some publications will print all of your speech; most will summarize. Draft press releases when you have important news to communicate and send them to your press contacts. Not all of your releases will be published, but many will. To increase your chances of getting your releases in print, make sure that your information is really news, and not just an obvious attempt to get free advertising. Keep your releases short and to the point, well-written and without error, factually correct, and timely. Make certain that the news won't be out of date once it is printed. Remember to mark your release with the date of issue and release date.

Include a photograph with your press release; doing so increases the probability of your press release being used by about 60 percent. If you do include a photo of yourself (in marketing promotions as well as press releases), use a professional photographer who specializes in executive portraiture. Do not try to save money with inexpensive home photography. A poor photo can do more harm than good.

Once your news and ideas begin to be seen in print, those in a position to refer or make use of your services directly will begin to notice that your thinking is of sufficient value to be regularly picked up and communicated by the press. This makes you of greater value in their minds, and they have greater confidence in retaining or recommending your services.

An added benefit from writing letters to the editor and press releases is that the press will begin to identify you as a valuable resource. Most members of the press maintain a file of resource contacts—people they view as knowledgeable who may be called upon for interpretation of news events or a quotation to use in connection with a story they are writing. Such names come from a variety of sources, but one of the most fruitful sources is names they see published in their own and other publications—people who have served as background sources in the past. Thus, your initial efforts to obtain press coverage beget more press coverage, and such additional press coverage begets even more. This is synergy. In a reasonably short time those prospects able to make use of your services or to refer you to others find that you have become almost a household name (in their area of need), resulting in even more business coming your way.

While press coverage provides excellent publicity for your services, it should never stand alone as a marketing strategy. Sending out press releases and writing letters to the editor should supplement and enhance other marketing techniques.

Q22
How can I use public speaking engagements to promote my professional services?

Making speeches and presentations to groups (such as trade and professional associations) that would be likely to have prospective clients as members can be a highly successful marketing strategy, increasing your visibility and enhancing your image as an authority in your field.

Develop three or more relatively short speeches and promote the availability of your services as a speaker to speakers' bureaus, associations, and corporate meeting planners. Your speech should not be highly technical, but it should provide practical information of interest to your audiences. Don't make your talk a sales pitch. You will do far better giving an informative speech and subtly promoting the availability of your professional services. Weave into your speech anecdotes, examples, and illustrations. In addition to making your speech more interesting and entertaining to listeners, such stories can relate information about your services and professional experience indirectly. Practice your speeches so that you appear comfortable, professional, and knowledgeable; convey to your audience that you are an experienced authority on your subject.

When making a speech or presentation, check out and arrange the facilities and equipment before you talk. Checking the microphone and slide projector and determining if there is a glass of water on the podium are not tasks that should be done after you have been introduced.

If you are to be introduced prior to a speech or participation in a panel discussion, always draft your own introduction and provide it to the person responsible for introducing you. Indicate that the introducer is free to say what he wants, but that other hosts have found having a prepared introduction useful for organizing their remarks. Don't make your introduction too lengthy. Provide it on a small, unobtrusive piece of paper and use type of sufficient size that it will be easy to read. Write it in newspaper (inverted pyramid) style, putting the most important information first and the less important information later, although it should close on an important high. Doing so permits you to control, or at least influence, what is said about you and how it is said.

And in situations where it is comfortable and appropriate, write a closing or thank you for the remarks that you have made. Many hosts fumble for appropriate words to say at the close. You will make them more comfortable and be able to communicate the kind of information that will lead to business opportunities and referrals.

In addition, when speaking before a group, avoid setting out a stack of your brochures (capability statements) that you hope the audience will pick up and read. Instead, during your talk, mention a valuable information product or item you will be pleased to send to people who leave a business card. This permits you to follow up personally with each and to add their names to your mailing list for future contact. Just as you are concluding your remarks, remind the audience to leave their business cards if they want the free copy of _____. As an added benefit, your host or sponsor will see that the group is so motivated by your words that they rush up and surround you when you have finished speaking. This increases the probability that you will be asked back next time.

In addition to giving a great talk that is truly helpful and informative, be sure to communicate your accessibility for future contact. All who hear you speak should leave with the feeling that they would be perfectly comfortable picking up the telephone the next day and giving you a call. They should not feel that doing so will cause you to start the meter and send an invoice for services.

Q23
How can I identify public-speaking opportunities?

There are, according to experts in the lecture bureau business, more than 9,000 opportunities in North America to give a lecture or a speech each day. If you have ever been a member of the program committee of a trade or professional association committee—worse yet, if you've been chairperson of the committee—you know how difficult it is for these organizations to identify and book relevant, meaningful speakers who can say something of interest and of value to the membership. Accordingly, you will find the demand for quality speakers great.

To identify organizations that would welcome you as a speaker, you should be familiar with the *Encyclopedia of Associations* (Gale Research Company, Book Tower, Detroit, MI 48226), which has both a national and a regional edition. These books contain the listings of the headquarters of trade, technical, and professional organizations. There are more than 15,000 organizations: Take a look at your particular area of specialization in these directories to discover speaking opportunities. Contact the national headquarters of those organizations, identify the local chapters, and volunteer yourself as a speaker. You will find that there is ample opportunity to give speeches, talks, and presentations to these groups. There are breakfast meetings, luncheon meetings, dinner meetings; there are quarterly meetings, semiannual meetings, monthly meetings, annual meetings. The people who attend—as opposed to those who simply pay their dues and stay home—are ideal prospects for your services because they need information and help; they are looking for communication with people who can assist them in solving their problems. By providing relevant, interesting, valuable information in your speeches, you will build a strong professional reputation rapidly, and you'll gain clients.

In addition to the national, trade, technical, and professional organizations, there are corporate meetings and civic, business, and community groups: Rotary, Lions, Kiwanis, Chamber of Commerce, Better Business Bureau, etc. The members of such organizations could also be potential clients; thus, it is to your benefit to identify these additional opportunities and offer your speaking services to them as well.

Q24

Is giving seminars a viable means of building my professional image and marketing my services?

The adult education business is one of the fastest-growing industries in North America today, and it's quite likely to continue to expand at a rapid rate. People have more leisure time, technology is changing, and information is advancing. While there are numerous ways to obtain information, seminars are particularly attractive because they allow participants to obtain desired knowledge quickly, in organized and strategically encapsulated form. Developing and/or conducting seminars of interest to your prospective clients will gain you exposure to a great number of people who are in a position to make use of your professional services—and can be profitable as well.

You can either sponsor your own seminars or find an external sponsor. It is usually not in your interest to solicit teaching assignments from regular academic departments of colleges and universities. Most are adequately staffed and the repetition of meeting with the same prospects over time is of less benefit than one-shot seminar appearances for generating potential business opportunities. But do talk to the deans and directors of continuing and extension education; they sponsor numerous seminars and short courses. And be creative by talking to those whom most don't consciously regard as being in the seminar and workshop business: Churches are moving heavily into secular education, chambers of commerce now give workshops, and the Y's are a major forum for seminars. Even department stores are involved; major chains now give in-store seminars and workshops, developed and conducted by outside professionals. And, of course, there are hundreds of proprietary seminar companies, such as the American Management Association, CareerTrack, Fred Proyor Seminars, seeking talented developers and presenters.

Give some thought, if you don't find the right sponsor, to sponsoring your own seminar or workshop. Whether you charge a fee or offer a free seminar, conducting such programs will bring to you people who are potentially interested in your services.

Once you have elected to take advantage of this rapidly expanding market opportunity and have chosen a topic relevant to your professional services, how do you ensure success? Here are seven guidelines for developing and presenting an effective seminar or workshop:

1. Determine your objectives. What specifically do you want your participants to be able to do after attending your program? Write one sentence describing your overall objective and then list the specific skills and/or knowledge that your participants will possess at the conclusion of your program.

2. Use a variety of strategies to get your participants actively involved. Researchers have found that people remember approximately 10 percent of what they read, 20 percent of what they hear, 40 percent of what they see and hear, and up to 90 percent of what they do. Actively involving your participants will ensure a more effective learning experience. Brainstorming, discussion, role play, and simulation are all effective techniques for active participation.

3. Create a step-by-step plan of action that will ensure your participants' success when followed. Seminars are often long on generalities and painfully short on the specific, how-to information that can spell the difference between success and failure. By supplying your participants with straightforward strategies and procedures that they can use as guides, you help them to implement your advice.

4. List the documents and other resources that your participants need in order to reach their objectives. As part of their seminar package, supply participants with sample documents and lists of recommended resources (people, organizations, suppliers, and additional information sources).

5. For each key point you wish to cover, provide at least one example from your own experience or the experience of others to illustrate the point. Intersperse such illustrations throughout your presentation. One good example is worth a thousand words of theoretical explanation, making your program more entertaining, meaningful, and memorable for participants.

6. Construct a detailed outline. Schedule each section of your seminar and stick to your schedule. Avoid too much detail in your outline; you don't need a word-for-word script, but at a minimum you should include time allotted, activities, and topics covered in each section of your program.

7. Polish your presentation skills. Once you have rehearsed your presentation, give it in front of a small group of

supportive colleagues and solicit their feedback. Videotape a segment of your seminar; examine your gestures, verbal delivery (pac-
ing, clarity, tone), eye contact, and mannerisms. Look for strengths
and weaknesses. You'll be surprised how quickly your skills will
improve when you use this simple tape feedback technique. Study
the delivery of accomplished speakers. Rehearse but don't memo-
rize; you want to be prepared but not stiff.

Q25
What are the benefits of publishing a newsletter?

There are more than 50,000 newsletters published in North America. Many of them are given away free, but a great many of them
are sold on a subscription basis. A newsletter is an excellent way
for you to increase your visibility and enhance your credibility as
an authority to your potential market while subtly promoting your
services. It can also enable you to provide a great deal of professional information to large numbers of people at low cost to both
you and your readers.

   According to recent research, the typical business executive
receives approximately 120 to 160 pieces of direct mail promotion
each week, both at home and at the office. Now what happens to
those 120 to 160 pieces of mail? Approximately half of them are
thrown out, prior to being opened or read, by someone other than
the executive, perhaps by a spouse or secretary. About half of the
remaining 70 are thrown out by the executive, either before or in
the process of being opened. You do that yourself—you slit open
the envelope, take a quick look, and, finding no check, toss it in the
trash. Of the remaining 35, 20 receive less than eight seconds of
attention before they're discarded. If your direct mail happens to
be one of the surviving 15, it will receive something more than
eight seconds of attention. Indeed it may get a thorough reading.
You may have people contact you. So if you send a typical brochure
through the mail, you have about a 10 percent chance that it's
going to be read. If, however, you send a newsletter with well-written, high-impact, detailed information, which would allow the
recipients to do a better job at whatever it is they do, you are almost
certainly going to be in the 10 percent that gets through. Even if

your newsletter is not read immediately, it's going to be put in a pocket or on a stack of things to be read and will be reviewed later.

You can subtly promote your services in the newsletter. Don't run full-page ads—that would make the newsletter look like a piece of direct mail promotion. You can, however, indirectly suggest to readers that you're in business to help them. Use examples from your professional experience to illustrate the descriptions, analysis, and discussion in your newsletter, thus letting people know about the work you do and the information you can provide.

Quite a few professionals develop a newsletter as a means of marketing themselves and then discover that it can become a very viable business opportunity, making someplace between $10,000 and $15,000 on the low side and upwards of $80,000 to $90,000 a year on the high side, simply by marketing a newsletter that also serves to market their services and build a stronger and better client base. If you can get your marketing done effectively and also be paid for doing it, that's not a bad expenditure of time and money.

Q26
How do I develop and publish a newsletter?

Once you decide to create a newsletter, you must determine your readers and/or market. If your newsletter is a promotional vehicle for developing your practice, prospects for your services will also be prospective readers of your newsletter. And, eventually, if your newsletter is successful, your readers will become your clients.

To target your market and to develop a topic for your newsletter, you should take a look at existing publications and newsletters. Spend time at a major library examining publication indexes—particularly *The Directory of Newsletters* (Howard Penn Hudson, Newsletter Clearinghouse, 44 West Market Street, Post Office Box 311, Rhinebeck, NY 12572), the *Oxbridge Directory of Newsletters*, and *The Standard Periodical Directory* (Oxbridge Communications, Inc., 150 Fifth Avenue, New York, NY 10011)—and write to the publishers of publications in your field to obtain sample copies. A complete absence of publications in a given field may indicate a ripe market, but more often it means that newsletters have not been very successful there in the past. However, a field in which a fair number of publications exist usually suggests a viable market, particularly if you can identify voids in the information being provided.

Selecting the market and selecting the topic are closely related. Whatever the topic of your newsletter, it should be very narrow, dealing with a specific group and a specific kind of information or problem. It might deal with judicial decisions in a particular field, new or pending legislation, governmental regulations, new products or literature, or perhaps research advances. Remember, however, that unless your newsletter is to serve as an alternative means of delivering professional services, it should not be so detailed and specific as to provide free information to readers that would make your professional services unnecessary. The more specialized the newsletter is, the better it will be read, the more helpful it will be to the reader; hence, the more your reputation will be enhanced and the more clients you will gain.

Before you begin writing, you must establish what subject(s) most interest(s) your readers and limit yourself to it. The trick to success is to have more news than you could possibly know what to do with.

Pay attention to "people news." People are gossips; they want to know who was hired, fired, demoted, promoted, awarded, etc. Ask your readers to send you news. They are a great source of information and most will enjoy the opportunity to assist you (and to see their news in print). In addition, interview prominent individuals in your field and newsmakers who have an impact on it. Interviewees usually are pleased to be covered in the press, to obtain free publicity, and you and your newsletter will get publicity when they photocopy it to give to friends and associates (so make sure that every page of the newsletter contains the name and address of the publication).

You can also obtain news from additional sources:

Newspapers, magazines, and other newsletters
Press releases
Copies of speeches
Government, university, and research institute monographs
   and research reports

Clipping services
Congressional and legislative digests
Trade and professional association reports

When you are ready to begin writing, select some regular categories of news that you will feature in every issue; for example, industry meetings, seminars and workshops, conventions and trade shows, people news, financial and merger news, new products, legislation, judicial decisions, etc. Devote space to each category, and rank the news items within each in terms of their importance to your readers. Then sit down and begin rewording or interpreting the news. One effective and often used approach is to present the news item in regular type and follow it with a paragraph of interpretation in italics.

The abundance of news versus the limitation of space will force you to be concise and to the point. Use a catchy, quick writing style. Space is dear and you have a lot of information to communicate, so formal writing isn't expected or required; however, accuracy of content and correct spelling and grammar are.

With the availability of desktop publishing equipment and software, you can design and lay out your newsletter yourself (it need not be typeset unless you want it to be) and then have it printed. Keep the design and format simple. It should suggest that the news is informative and up-to-date. Easy-to-read type, black print on good quality white paper with a single additional color (for emphasis) if desired, and simple graphics should be ideal.

If you publish a newsletter, you need a mailing list; the names in your Rolodex or personal phone book are a good way to start. Most of these people are prospective clients or referral sources for your services, so be sure to send them the newsletter. But don't stop with these 50, 100, or 150 people; there are many others you will want to contact. An excellent way to get in touch with additional candidates for your newsletter, and thus your services, is to rent mailing lists. Standard Rate and Data Service (SRDS, Inc., Macmillan Inc., 3004 Glenview Road, Wilmette, IL 60091) publishes a number of directories for the marketing field that can be found in most major libraries. One such directory is *Direct Mail Lists Rates and Data*, which is updated every two months. It contains listings and descriptions, and provides the rental fee for more than 50,000 North American direct mail marketing lists.

Placing small space ads in daily newspapers, magazines, and journals is sometimes the most effective promotion technique. In such an ad, provide the reader with the opportunity to obtain a free copy of your newsletter by writing to you, and then send a sample along with information about yourself, the benefits of the newsletter, and how to become a subscriber.

You may find it best to give away your newsletter without charge. Of course, you can charge a subscription price based on what the market will bear. For some professionals a newsletter becomes an important profit center as well as a good self-promotion device. If you don't charge for it, people will begin to contact you, asking to be put on the mailing list, or complaining: you were late this month; page four was smudged; send me another copy. This should be a very clear indication to you that your newsletter has value in its own right—as well as in promoting your professional services—and you can begin charging for it.

If you charge for your newsletter, you will discover that some who would like to read it won't be willing to pay. As a newsletter publisher, you are not precluded from sending out copies for free to certain readers—perhaps the best prospects for your services or influential members of the press.

Q27
Will selling information products have a negative impact on my professional image?

Developing and marketing high-quality information products (newsletters, manuals, software, seminars, etc.) will increase the demand for your professional services, allow you to create sources of passive and accrual income, and have a positive impact on your professional stature.

Traditionally, professionals have expanded their practices by hiring lower cost professionals and billing their time at a rate greater than the cost of compensation. In many cases, such personnel are not staff, but independent subcontractors. In more recent times, many professionals—motivated to free themselves from organizational complexity and increasing supervisory responsibility—have found this conventional expansion approach less attractive.

The need to create income that is not dependent upon personal expenditure of time is a goal shared by vast numbers of professionals. Dentists are a good example. The very minute they stop drilling and filling, they have to stop billing. Hence, the traditional notion of making money off the labor of others has been appealing, despite the complexity and overhead it creates. Today, professionals have a new option: They can create information products—seminars, newsletters, training programs, databases, software, books, manuals, audio and videotapes, syndicated articles, etc., that permit a one-time expenditure of labor and the potential for producing long-term, accrual, and residual income.

The most successful professionals consistently devote time to developing such products based on their know-how. Some worry that the creation of a product will reduce demand for their professional services, but the evidence suggests quite the contrary:

1. Creating and marketing information products provides an easy way for potential clients to see what it's like to work with you and gain insight into the variety of ways you can be of help.

2. Few prospects are interested in spending their time being sold. Let the value of the information products be your silent seller. If prospects find your information products to be of value, they will be more inclined to seek you out to provide professional services.

3. Many professionals find soliciting for business makes them somewhat uncomfortable. Some even think it unprofessional. But marketing and selling activities to secure the sale of a product are both comfortable and expected. Brochures, advertisements, and other means used to generate product sales can indicate that professional services are available. And the opportunities to discuss such services later are obvious. In fact, your product sales literature and your one-on-one conversations can nicely include information on how such materials combine with your services and round out the total assistance that you make available.

4. For many professionals, direct marketing of services is unproductive and unprofitable. Such marketing can create the
impression of your being needy or hungry. Further, those who
may be interested are often reluctant to contact you out of fear
that your services will be costly or that simply discussing their
needs will result in an expensive fee. Marketing information
products provides a way for them to identify their needs or
interests. Potential clients and others willingly write and call
for information about products. Their interest often suggests a
possible need for professional services.

5. Some who could benefit from your services simply are not in a
financial position to retain you; later they may be. If they are
able to obtain the benefit of your expertise through information products that you have created and authored, they will be
indebted to you and may make use of your services in the
future.

6. Providing your clients with assistance in a more cost-efficient
form makes you a better professional. This becomes obvious to
your clients. Many professionals spend too much time communicating to clients information that is already available in
more economical form: books, software, databases, or videotapes. If clients recognize this, the professional's image can suffer. Thus, those advisors who restrict professional services to
areas where no more efficient information is available tend to
be more credible and usually have far more interesting (and
profitable) practices.

7. Marketing and selling information products is profitable, providing income independent of time expended. Failure to do so
robs your practice of a meaningful source of revenue.

Those who create and effectively market information products
increase demand for their services; they are better known and
achieve greater recognition as authorities. More prospects for their
services become aware of their capabilities and seek them out, and
those unable to afford the fee for their services now can purchase
their products. In time the successes achieved from the products
make these buyers superior prospects for professional or consulting
services. And the professionals are able to return to doing their

highest and best work: performing creative, leading-edge services for their clients.

> If you are having trouble convincing prospects of the wisdom of your ideas and making use of your services, your marketing may be too rational. We sometimes think selling professional services to the business market is a totally rational sell. It isn't always. Your marketing may have to appeal to the nonrational needs of the prospect, with particular emphasis on how making use of your services will benefit the prospect personally.

3

REFERRAL MARKETING: Making Your Practice Grow through Referrals and Recommendations

There is probably no more rewarding approach to marketing professional services than to receive referral business—clients to whom you have been recommended by past, prospective, and existing clients, colleagues, friends, and others—or follow-up business from existing clients. Nor is there a more cost-effective form of marketing. Unfortunately, many consultants just wait for it to happen, and unless you take action to create and facilitate referrals, they will be few and far between.

The most successful professionals know that referrals and recommendations are the best source of new client business. The more referral and follow-up business you receive, the faster your practice will grow and the greater the profitability you will achieve.

Many consultants look at referral business as coming exclusively from former clients. Former clients, however, are only one source of referrals. Current clients are in an even better position to recommend you because they tend to interact daily with others who have problems similar to theirs and who are as much in need of your services. Don't forget former business associates, professional associates, past employers, etc., whom you have served or worked with well or who have evidence that you do good and creative work.

Social contacts are not a primary or even a particularly good source of referrals for most professionals. Some, however, have a lifestyle that makes social contacts a very fertile source. Bankers, financial administrators, financial finders, and consultants often come in contact with many people who need a variety of skills, including those which you have to offer. Politicians and governmental administrators, your competitors, your professional peers—the business community at large—are an excellent source of recommendation and referral if they are handled properly. They too are in a position to refer business your way and will often do so even if they have not had personal contact with you—given that they have knowledge of your reputation and skills.

However, many in a position to refer you may be reluctant to do so. Some do not trust their ability to evaluate the quality of your skills and services. They may think that you are good, professional, and ethical, but they lack confidence in their own judgment. They are afraid that they will recommend you to others who will find you unsatisfactory or unsuitable, and as a result will cast doubt on the quality of their evaluations, their decision-making, or their motivations for referring you.

Others are fearful about your ethics and professional behavior. You may be very good at what you do, but perhaps they have had no recent contact with you or have never had direct contact. They may be afraid that if you're looking for business, seeking referrals, perhaps things are not going as well for you as they once were, and that may have compromised your professional behavior or your ethics. And so, they don't make the referral because they don't want to chance hurting their own image and reputation.

There's also the "I don't want to get involved" syndrome: People tend not to want to extend themselves beyond what is necessary. And some are afraid that if they recommend you, particularly to their colleagues or competitors, you may disclose sensitive, proprietary, or personal information about the person who made the referral.

Many more do not refer you because they simply do not know how to go about it correctly and professionally. No one, including you, has shown them how they can help you—specifically, how they can handle the referral.

But the majority of people who realize and appreciate the quality and value of your services do want to refer, despite the fears or reasons they might have for not recommending you. Perhaps they want to do you a favor because of some assistance you provided or services you performed, or because they think highly of you. For whatever reasons, people like to do favors, and therefore, would like to be able to refer you, particularly if they can minimize their risks. They also want to assist those to whom they're referring you. If Client A recommends you to Client B and Client B is satisfied, Client A derives a certain esteem, certain benefits, from Client B that are to Client A's advantage.

Moreover, people like to be admired and to feel that their opinions, judgment, and ideas are valued. They also want to be thought of as powerful and influential. Having others come to them for recommendations and advice is a strong motivation for them to refer. Thus, it is greatly to your advantage to develop strategies and a philosophy for facilitating referrals and follow-up business. Of course, most of all, you must provide superlative services to your clients for reasonable fees to make them want to refer you. Keep clients advised of what you're doing, even after finishing the project, so that when they know someone in need of the services you provide, your name is the first to come to mind. Without seeming anxious or in need of the business, you must make clients, colleagues, and others aware that you very much appreciate and benefit from referrals, and you must subtly direct them; show them how to make the most professional and productive referrals that benefit everyone—the person making the referral, the individuals to whom they are recommending your services, and you.

The rewards of a good referral marketing system are great. However, private practice has its ups and downs, and you should not allow yourself to become complacent. Renew your good fortune by continuing to employ the strategies that make you successful. And as you obtain more and better clients as a result of your referral marketing efforts, remember to exhibit the very same standards of professionalism, good taste, courtesy, and ethics that produce the benefits you enjoy. Avoid behavior that smacks of self-importance; you cannot afford to be cavalier or impolite. As a close friend is fond of saying, "Be nice to people on your way up because you will meet the very same people on your way down."

Q28
What tactics can I use to stimulate follow-on business and referrals?

The best strategy to make clients call you back and refer you to others is to provide superb service. To that end, here are a few suggestions that have proven to help:

1. Don't turn an assignment into an ego trip. Make the client and the client's staff look good.

2. Don't raise expectations by making casual promises. Clients listen hard to any communications that suggest "results and outcomes." Be careful that the euphoria of the moment doesn't cause you to have to backpedal later.

3. Avoid making decisions for the client. Develop the art and science of staging decisions; show clients how decisions should be made, but take care not to usurp the client's authority.

4. Don't become visibly upset or functionally rattled when clients drop the ball. They will. Coolly and rationally explain the problems that have been created by the client's lack of activity or action, and demonstrate an easy way for the client to accomplish what is necessary to get the project back on track.

5. Don't turn the professional relationship into a social one (at least while rendering services for the client). It's okay to be a friend, but being a friend is not your primary role. Friendship should never interfere with your mission.

6. Be timely in communicating bad news. Most clients don't shoot the messenger.

7. Train your client and the client's staff to be self-sufficient. The best business comes from clients who no longer need you to do repetitive tasks and are now able to have you engage in more creative and productive work.

8. Document what you have done for your clients and provide them with meaningful progress reports (oral and/or written) that cause them to see the wisdom and cost efficiency of having made use of your services.

9. Be courageous and decisive.

10. Be open and accessible to your client and the client's staff.

11. Admit mistakes and errors in judgment.

12. Devote time on a regular basis to identifying problems in the client organization that need attention (maybe your attention) and communicate the nature of the problem and a recommended solution or approach that your client will see as reasonable and affordable.

13. Devote time on a regular basis to developing the skills and decision-making ability of your client and the client's staff.

14. Reduce the threat to staff members in the client's organization by working through them and not at their expense.

15. Do things the way your client would do them to create an environment of comfort and acceptability.

16. Listen and read between the lines to uncover latent client dissatisfaction with the services being provided, the fees being charged, and the progress being made.

17. Don't undertake projects that are outside your area of expertise or beyond your ability to deliver.

18. Avoid the halo syndrome. Just because you have done one or several things successfully for a client does not mean that you

can do everything, even though they think you can. Learn when to say no!

19. Don't become overinvested in your solutions. Even the best advisors learn from their experiences and their clients.

20. Be firm on business matters such as getting contracts signed and invoices paid. Your client will respect you more.

21. Know the value of additional and better information. Don't suffer decision-making or decision-staging paralysis, waiting for information that isn't really needed or for which the value is less than the cost of indecision.

22. Promote yourself, subtly, in the client's organization when you deserve it.

23. Don't blame others for lack of progress. Point out early the obstacles to your success, and direct your client on strategies to be implemented to run interference for you.

24. Give your clients well over 100 percent. Let them discover for themselves that you are not only effective but a good investment.

Q29
What's the best way to act on a referral from a client?

The next time a client or anyone else says, "I know someone who would benefit from your services, why don't you give him a call, and feel free to use my name," don't call!

Wait for the person to call you. If you think this is a professional referral, you are wrong. Properly handled, it can become one. But it is not professional for you to call, because it puts you in the position of soliciting business. How would you feel if an architect, lawyer, doctor, or accountant called and said, "I hear you have a need for my services"?

But how can you ensure that the person will call? You must take steps to have the person who is attempting to network the two of you do so properly. For example:

1. Tell the networker that you would be pleased to discuss the needs of the person who might benefit from your services, and

ask the networker to tell the individual to please feel free to call you. Alternatively, suggest that the three of you get together for lunch.

2.   Discuss, with the networker, the prospect's needs in greater detail and indicate that you have some information (an article, a paper, a reprint, etc.) that might be useful. Then forward the material to the networker with a letter that says, in part, "I think that the enclosed information will be beneficial to Mr./ Ms. _____; please feel free to make it available to him/her." Or, if you feel that the referring source will not follow through, send the information directly to the prospect with a letter that says "Mr. Y thought that the enclosed material would be beneficial to you and has requested that I provide it for your review. Please feel free to contact me if I may provide additional information." Do not directly pitch your services.

3.   Explain to the networker that you do not solicit business but that he should feel free to have the prospect contact you. Then, find a reason to call the prospect in the next few days to obtain his ideas on the subject in connection with the continuing research you are doing in that area. It is acceptable to indicate that Mr. Y told you that this is an area in which the prospect is interested/knowledgeable/experienced.

Success in obtaining referrals depends critically upon showing people willing and able to refer how to do so. To be effective, a professional referral must be handled in a very precise, strategic, and sophisticated fashion. Many who would be happy to refer do not do so because they lack comfort with or knowledge of the mechanics of the process. Show them how to do so in a way that makes them able to refer with finesse. Since each potential referral source is different, there is not one "educational message" that is effective in all situations. You must tailor the means of referral to each referring party's needs. One professional explains to those in need two or three examples of how referrals should and should not be made. She does not do this in a way that might communicate a selfish purpose, but as a means of general education and development for her clients that will likely benefit her later.

Keep those who have referred in the communication loop. Obviously, it isn't appropriate to communicate details or confidences related to the services you have provided. But an occasional follow-up telephone call or letter informing the source of the referral about how well it is working for both your client and for you will stimulate future referrals and is simply common courtesy.

Q30
What percentage of my business can I expect to generate from referrals?

A creative professional should be able to derive 80 percent or more of all new business from referrals. Experience in working with many thousands of professionals strongly suggests that a reliance on tips and techniques will not be productive. Obtaining abundant, quality referral business is the result of efforts undertaken to develop and implement a carefully crafted strategy and philosophy.

To help communicate the distinction between strategy-philosophy and tip-technique let me share an experience. On numerous occasions, I have been asked by professionals to share with them tips to get past secretaries and other palace guards to obtain unchallenged access to decision-makers. Often, these questioners seek evaluation of some supposedly effective technique—calling before 8:00 A.M. when no secretary is at work, for example. Having never experienced difficulty obtaining access to any decision-maker, I find such questions somewhat curious.

In probing the nature of their difficulty, it generally becomes obvious that their problem is attributable to the fact that they have nothing of value or substance to communicate in the first place. Palace guards are implanted in executive offices for just this reason—to ensure that valuable time is not wasted with unimportant communications. If the professional would only communicate a message of significance, access would not be blocked.

In the same sense, building a viable referral marketing program will not be well served by tips and techniques. The professional must create a philosophy and strategy that permeates the very nature of his or her practice. This is not to say that the professional won't employ various techniques or from time to time take advantage of tips successfully used by others.

An important motivation for developing a strong referral marketing system is not just to acquire new clients, but to develop your practice by obtaining better clients and more interesting and professionally challenging assignments. Even those with more business than they have time to handle have found it beneficial to expend great time and energy in referral marketing because experience has taught them that having the right clients has strong economic and professional advantages.

Don't postpone the development of a referral marketing system and strategy because you are too busy or too successful. Time and energy expended on developing a strong referral base will pay off handsomely, but the best results will accrue over time. The time to build a solid source of referrals is not when you need business, but when you don't.

Equip your practice to make referral marketing easy and creative. Many professionals who know the benefits of developing a good referral marketing system fail to do so because they lack internal systems that enable referrals to be implemented with ease and efficiency. Technology can make implementation of referral strategies relatively quick, easy, and cost-efficient. Developing or obtaining a computer-based client/prospect referral database, software program, etc., which allows you immediate access to needed information, could be the most important investment you make in business development.

Q31
How can I ensure that 80 percent of new business comes from referrals?

To be effective, a referral must be both compelling and enthusiastic. In motivating others to refer, you must not only engender an almost religious zeal about your abilities, but an equal faith in your ethics, standards, and values. Avoid any activity that detracts from your professionalism or that suggests that you are in need of the business that results from referrals received.

Others are motivated to refer business to you when they believe that your services are uniquely suited to the precise needs and expectations of the person to whom the referral is being made. Thus, your communications (letters, conversations, brochures, etc.) must be specific and tailored. Reliance on general, "fits-any-purpose" communications will rarely be productive. You must convince the referring party that you are the only one, or at least one of a handful of people, uniquely suited to be of value. Developing and conveying such specialized communications is more time-consuming, but generally well worth the effort.

Many in a position to make referrals lack confidence in their ability to measure accurately your value to those to whom they might recommend your services. Referral marketing will be greatly assisted by allowing those in a position to refer to rely on external sources able to corroborate their perception of your value. You should expend significant energy in building a public aura about your talents. The fact that many have great conviction about your abilities reduces the fear referral sources have about their ability to judge your value.

Referrals are made to those who are perceived as giving and not just taking. You should be perceived by others as a meaningful, contributing member of the profession, not just someone seeking to profit. Generous and significant contributions in the form of publishing information; participating in industry and/or professional, educational, and research endeavors; assisting the less fortunate in ways appropriate to your abilities, etc., help create an environment that encourages referrals.

The referring party must perceive that the party to whom the referral is made will benefit at least as much as and preferably more than you. Significant referrals that produce results are rarely made if the referring source has any reason to believe that you are in need of the business that might result. Your marketing efforts must clearly communicate an air of indifference about whether you obtain the business. Obviously, those who refer know, in a general sense, that you need business, but they cannot conclude that the specific business that would result from their referral is essential for your continued economic viability. Your marketing efforts must convince them that you are busy, successful, and in demand.

No matter how great your abilities and talents, people will not refer good business to you if they have any doubt about your ethics or professionalism. It is vital that you avoid any activity that detracts from your professional image. For example, you should never disclose information about clients or others that might be regarded as proprietary or confidential. And you should never engage in marketing practices that might cause others to question your ethics. The definition of ethical marketing behavior varies by field of specialization and is modified over time, but you are best to err on the side of good taste.

It is not likely that referrals will be made, or at least made consistently, unless you make known to those in a position to refer that you would find their referral advantageous. While it may seem obvious to you that everyone should know that you would benefit from and appreciate referrals, many don't usually devote effort to your well-being unless prompted to do so. Thus, you must find a comfortable and professional way of communicating your desire to be the recipient of referrals (without appearing in need of business). Some are comfortable being rather direct in such matters. Others are not. If you are not, find a way of subtly communicating your interest. One professional always takes time to explain, indirectly, how referrals are the lifeblood of her business. In essence, she plants the seed of suggestion and allows it to mature and bear fruit.

Referrals are indeed the lifeblood of professional practice. A creative professional or consultant who offers quality services should be able to derive 80 percent or more of all new business from referrals. Learning, practicing, and perfecting referral-garnering strategies will be well worth your effort.

Q32
Should I give gifts as thanks for referrals?

Consider carefully both the issue of bestowing gifts and the nature of any gifts given to those whom you want to thank for providing referrals. While spoken thanks convey immediate appreciation,

> Encourage multiple referrals. Hearing from just one source that you are good at what you do may be encouraging to a prospective client. However, hearing the same message from two or three sources is convincing. Whenever possible, orchestrate multiple (and always genuine) recommendations of your services to a targeted prospect.

they are insufficient. At the least, the receipt of a referral should be promptly acknowledged with a written communication expressing thanks and emphasizing the potential benefits for your new client vis-à-vis how it will enrich your personal well-being. Such a thank you may be all that is necessary or appropriate.

You may also want to provide the referring source with a gift. Remember: In certain circumstances, in certain fields, a present may not be viewed as appropriate, ethical, or acceptable. Any gift should be selected with great care. It should be something of a value that would never cause the recipient or others (particularly your new client) to think that the referral was motivated by the expectation or value of the gift. Beyond these considerations, choose the present with concern for the special interests and tastes of the referring party.

While the receipt of a referral should be acknowledged in writing immediately, providing a gift might best be delayed. If the present is a specific follow-up to the receipt of a referral, it should be forwarded promptly. But often a gift given later may have greater impact. Such a gift need not be of obvious commercial or material value, or a one-for-one recognition. An occasional remembrance acknowledging your appreciation for those who have benefited you may be most effective.

Creativity in selecting the most appropriate acknowledgment of a referral can significantly (and quite favorably) affect the generation of future referrals. For example, one highly regarded professional hosts a twice-yearly weekend at resorts, ski lodges, hunting lodges, etc. All expenses are paid and those invited to participate (about eight to twelve each time) are provided with two to three days of accommodations, food, spirits, and recreation. Dur-

Remember, prospects for your services are referral sources and vice versa. You may view as a referral source someone who might also be a prospect for your services directly. And someone whom you have categorized as a potential client may never engage your services but become a bountiful source of referrals. Don't be too quick to categorize and don't forget that some you think of as prospects will be unwilling to make use of your services until they have had the opportunity to refer you and obtain an evaluation from the party to whom they have made the referral.

ing these weekends, several hours in 1½- to 2½-hour segments are devoted to intellectual and professional pursuits tied closely to the host's expertise. Not only is it an enjoyable experience, but it also benefits the host by providing him with an opportunity to share his latest creative thinking and ideas. The guests are individuals who have been exceptionally good clients, fertile sources of referral business, and others to whom the host feels a professional indebtedness.

In choosing gifts to acknowledge the receipt of referrals, be sure not to start something you will later not be in a position to continue. This is a good policy to follow for all gift giving. One professional sent a tasteful and uncompromising gift after the

As your expertise in obtaining good referrals increases and the number of potential referral sources grows, you may find it both efficient and effective to divide your potential referral sources into two or more categories. Certainly you will find it useful to have an A list and a B list and perhaps C and D lists as well. The nature, frequency, and type of interactions and communications with those on the lists may be quite different. And nothing precludes you from moving an A list entry to the B list and vice versa as circumstances and experience dictate.

receipt of a referral but sent nothing in response to the second one. The absence of a gift for the second referral stood out much more prominently. Another individual, who sent a Christmas present for three years, reverted to sending just a card. The recipients wonder whether their business and/or referrals have become expected or less important and, thus, unworthy of as meaningful an acknowledgment and appreciation.

4

DIRECT MARKETING: Using Advertising and Brochures to Promote Your Practice

While indirect, public-relations types of marketing strategies tend to produce the most and best prospects for professionals, direct marketing (for example, brochures, advertisements, sales letters) can be effective as well, particularly if used in conjunction with more subtle promotional efforts.

As with any promotion, the purpose of direct marketing is to persuade potential clients to contact you so that you can communicate the benefits of your services. Given the time, it would be ideal to write every prospective client an individualized letter tailored to that client's interests and needs. Indeed, when most consultants begin practice, they have yet to write a brochure or capabilities statement, so when prospects ask to receive information, beginning professionals tend to write letters that dovetail their skills and capabilities with each potential client's needs. The result is a highly effective sales letter suggesting that the consultant has a perceptive understanding of the client's problem and/or need and has the relevant experience for the assignment. Most professionals write a number of these highly effective and productive sales letters before finally realizing that they are too busy serving clients and pursuing other marketing efforts to communicate so specifically with every prospect who expresses interest in their services. It is only then that they take time to develop a brochure or capabilities statement.

A brochure by no means replaces the personalized letter or proposal. It does serve as a prelude or as a supplement to more specific and personalized marketing efforts. There are many instances in which an individualized letter would be unnecessary, inappropriate, or premature (such as when someone asks for information for another person whom you do not know; when you are giving speeches or presentations to a large group; when you meet prospects at a meeting/convention/workshop, at a social event, or on an airplane), but a capabilities statement would be ideal. Casual encounters with people who express interest in what you do create the perfect excuse to send a brochure describing your expertise, skills, and services and promoting your availability and accessibility. Given knowledge of you and your services and provided with the opportunity to get in touch with you for further information, many of these casual contacts will become prospects for your services, and many of the prospects will become clients.

A brochure or capabilities statement is not an effective primary marketing tool and should not be viewed as such. However, properly written and effectively distributed, it can make a strong contribution to the growth, success, and profitability of your practice.

So, too, can the right advertising. Direct advertising is a relatively new phenomenon for professional practitioners. In the past, it was often viewed as unprofessional or unethical to advertise professional services. However, that view is rapidly changing, and it has become quite common in many fields for professionals to advertise their services. When deciding whether or not advertising is appropriate for marketing your services, you should consider how other professionals in your field and geographic area promote their services.

If you elect to advertise, you should be as specific as possible to make the most of your marketing dollars. Effective advertising does not result from designing a tombstone or business card ad. It is essential to determine your market first—to target the ideal prospects for your services and then design a highly specific advertisement that appeals to that limited audience. While such an ad will not appeal to large numbers, it will have high impact on the target you have identified. Your advertisement must be direct enough to stimulate the interest and curiosity of your best potential clients and to persuade them to contact you for further information. Determine what would be most attractive to your target market—perhaps an offer for free information of interest to them (a research report, survey, small booklet, etc.)—and design your ad around that. When prospects respond to the ad, you can send the requested information along with literature that will cause them to see the benefits of making use of your services.

If you decide to advertise in print media, is it more effective to advertise in newspapers or in magazines and journals? If the services you provide appeal to a very general audience or to one so specialized that there is no more efficient way to reach it (perhaps there are no good trade publications or comprehensive mailing lists available), you may want to place your advertisement in newspapers. However, if your market is more tightly targeted and well-defined and there are existing publications in the field, you would probably do better to advertise in the trade, professional, and technical journals and magazines that your prospects read.

Obtain copies of all the publications you are considering; the publisher or publisher's advertising representatives will be happy to supply you with a media kit and copies of the publication. When you're evaluating a newspaper, magazine, or journal, look at the other advertisements (as well as the features and articles) and see who's advertising to determine whether the publication and its readers are appropriate for the services you are promoting.

Success in designing and writing brochures and advertisements lies in being highly specific and in testing all facets (message, graphics, size, typeface, headlines, offer, etc.) of the promotion. Even if your marketing piece seems effective and productive, continue to test, revise, change, add, subtract, and perfect so that your brochure or ad remains fresh and innovative. Remember to stand back from it and continually ask yourself, "What is it that I do or could do that is of interest and of benefit to my market, and how can I package what I do in a way that will attract the best prospects for my services?" The answer becomes the focus of your marketing campaign and also causes you to concentrate on providing and promoting benefits to potential clients, instead of just going out and saying, "I have these skills. What can I do for you?"

Direct mail is the most widely used direct marketing strategy employed by professionals. It should be tested very carefully. The vast majority of professionals find that marketing professional services through cold mailings is both inefficient and ineffective. A few report excellent results. If you plan to do a cold direct mail solicitation, test small mailings (perhaps as small as a few hundred pieces) to obtain a feeling for whether larger mailings will be profitable.

To achieve a vital, successful, and profitable professional practice never become complacent in your marketing efforts.

Q33
Won't advertising my services create the impression that I'm in need of business and unsuccessful?

Advertising your professional services directly may give the impression that you are hungry or needy for clients. This is hardly the image you want to convey, since no one wants to do business with someone desperately in need of business. Yet the right advertising is generally very good for business. Most professionals benefit from indirect advertising far more than they do from a direct promotion of their services. Consider, for example, developing and advertising a booklet or pamphlet containing information that would be of value to the people whom you would like to have as clients. You can make a subtle pitch in the booklet that your services are available. (See Figures 4-1, 4-2, and 4-3.)

Figure 4-1   Sample advertisement offering a free booklet.

Don't hesitate to charge a small amount for your booklet. It serves as a screening device, since someone unwilling to pay a few dollars for valuable information is unlikely to pay your fee for professional services.

Your booklet should not only supply useful, specific information but should also illustrate the ways in which you could be helpful to readers (prospects). The pitch for your services, however, should be indirect. For example, you can raise several issues that cannot be answered in the booklet—perhaps because they are beyond its scope or because they are current information that would quickly outdate the booklet—and suggest that readers feel free to contact you if you can be of assistance in providing further information on the issues. Thus, you offer them the opportunity to contact you with no obligation, producing a great number of phone calls. A good number of those phone calls will result in face-to-face meetings. And a high percentage of those meetings will result in your obtaining a client.

Q34
Can "cold" direct mail promotion really produce clients?

Rarely! A few professionals have had acceptable to outstanding success in renting mailing lists of likely prospects and sending them either a brochure or sales letter or both. But most have not generated sufficient response to even pay for the postage, much less the many other expenses associated with direct mail.

How To Get More & Better Referrals:

73 Proven Strategies

By Howard L. Shenson, CMC

HOWARD L. SHENSON, CMC
MARKETING AND MANAGEMENT CONSULTANT
20750 VENTURA BOULEVARD
WOODLAND HILLS, CALIFORNIA 91364

TELEPHONE (818) 703-1415

Figure 4-2 Front and back covers of a free booklet.

ALSO AVAILABLE...

101 Proven Strategies For Building A Successful Practice

Master proven marketing strategies. Based on field research. What works and why! $3. ($3.75 Canadian) plus applicable sales tax.

77 Proven Strategies To Increase Seminar & Workshop Profits

Strategies used by the most successful. Solid information on how to increase registrations and reduce expenses. $4 ($5 Canadian) plus applicable sales tax.

OBTAIN INFORMATION LIKE THIS ON A REGULAR BASIS...

If you have benefited from the type of information contained in How To Get More & Better Referrals, consider subscribing to *The Professional Consultant & Seminar Business Report*. Each month, Howard Shenson shares the very latest strategies and news vital for your business development activities. Annual subscription (12 issues), $96 ($120 Canadian).

Figure 4-2 (continued)

ABOUT THE AUTHOR

Howard L. Shenson is a Certified Management Consultant specializing in the marketing and management of professional practices. He has worked with consultants, attorneys, accountants, medical and dental professionals, architects and engineers, counselors, therapists, financial planners and other professionals.

He began his practice on a part time basis while serving in administrative and teaching positions at the University of Southern California and the California State University. In 1971 he resigned his position as Chair of the Management faculty at California State University, Northridge to commence full time practice.

The author of more than two dozen books, audio and video cassettes, he has published numerous articles in professional journals and trade magazines and is the editor/publisher of his own monthly newsletter. A frequent speaker before the national meetings of trade and professional societies, more than 100,000 have attended his seminars on professional practice marketing, seminar promotion and entrepreneurship.

Shenson's work has been the subject of more than 400 newspaper and magazine articles and 250 plus television and radio interviews. For information about his publications, seminars and newsletter, please call or write:

HOWARD L. SHENSON, CMC
MARKETING AND MANAGEMENT CONSULTANT
20750 VENTURA BOULEVARD
WOODLAND HILLS, CALIFORNIA 91364
TELEPHONE (818) 703-1415

Single copy price $5.00 ($6.25 Canadian)
Applicable sales tax must be added.
Discounts available on orders for 25 or more.
Custom imprinting available. Please inquire.

Figure 4-3   Inside front and back covers of booklet.

PUBLICATIONS BY HOWARD L. SHENSON

Listed below are publications available from Howard L. Shenson. Prices are in U.S. dollars. (A = audio tapes, A+ = audio tapes with manual, B = book or manual, I = assessment instrument, N = newsletter, V = video tapes).

Beyond Consulting: How To Develop & Market Information Products & Services [A+] $139
Complete Guide To Consulting Success [B] $69.95
Consultant's Guide To Fee Setting [B] $29
Consultant's Guide To Proposal Writing [B] $49
Consulting Handbook [B] $59
Entrepreneurial Style & Success Indicator (ESSI) [I] $15
Grantsmanship Consulting [A+] $109
How To Build A Lucrative Paid Speaking Business [A] $79
How To Build & Maintain Your Own Full-Time/Part-Time Consulting Practice [A+] $149 (Abridged edition $89)
How To Build A Profitable Consulting Practice, Volume 1 - Marketing [V] $49.95
How To Build A Profitable Consulting Practice, Volume 2 - Proposals, Fees, Contracts & Collections [V] $49.95
How To Create & Market A Successful Seminar Or Workshop [B] $29
How To Develop & Promote Profitable Seminars & Workshops [A+] $159 (Abridged edition $99)
How To Select, Manage & Compensate Consultants, Trainers & Professional Practitioners [B] $39
How To Start & Promote Your Own Newsletter [A+] $79
How To Strategically Negotiate The Consulting Contract [B] $39
Marketing Your Professional Services [A] $89
Professional Consultant & Seminar Business Report [N] $96, per year (12 issues)
Publishing Is Your Second Business [A+] $109
Selling Consulting Services Face-To-Face [A+] $119
Strategic Seminar & Workshop Marketing [B] $49

Please communicate orders to:

Howard L. Shenson, CMC
20750 Ventura Boulevard
Woodland Hills, CA 91364
Telephone: 818/703-1415

Please add applicable sales tax to all orders plus $4 per item for priority shipping (except [I] and [N]). If paying by VISA, Master or American Express include card number, expiration date and signature. Phone orders accepted.

In a survey of 887 professionals representing numerous specialties nationally, some revealing data was obtained about the effectiveness of such promotions.

Survey respondents were asked the following questions and provided the responses indicated.

1. Have you ever done a cold direct mail solicitation to strangers, mailing a brochure or sales letter requesting those interested in your services to contact you?

    Yes 87.5%

2. How would you rate the effectiveness of the last such cold direct mail solicitation that you did?

    Very effective 3.2%
    Somewhat effective 11.5%
    Not very effective 60.1%
    Very ineffective 25.2%

3. Are you planning to do another such cold direct mail solicitation within the next 90 days? (Asked only of those who answered yes to question number 1.)

    Yes, definitely 9.3%
    Maybe 18.4%
    Probably not 37.7%
    Definitely not 34.6%

The majority of the respondents found that cold direct mail promotion is seldom an effective means of marketing services and gaining clients.

However, if you still wish to try cold mailings of brochures and/or sales letters, be careful. Test such promotions in very small quantities. Like all promotional pieces, your cold mail promotion should:

1. Be of interest to your potential clients and of no interest to anyone else.

2. Ask your potential clients to take a small, inconsequential step or action that will be of benefit; for example, write or call for free information (perhaps a report on a subject of great interest to them).

3. Let your potential clients know that you are available to them. It should encourage them to contact you.

4. Be credible. The small, inconsequential step you are asking your prospects to take should be believable. Don't promise to give too much.

The following few tips can increase the cost-effectiveness and success of cold direct mail marketing campaigns:

1. **Try a self-mailer rather than a traditional letter or brochure in an envelope.** Advertising is often thrown out even before the envelope is opened. A self-mailer can at least be scanned before the recipient discards it.

2. **Omit business reply envelopes and cards.** People in business will respond anyway.

3. **Use a reply envelope, but not prepaid postage.** The cost of a postage stamp will not deter an interested prospect from contacting you.

4. **Mail less.** Fewer qualified prospects will generally be better than many unqualified ones.

5. **Don't clean rented lists. Skip return postage, address correction, and forwarding on rented lists.** It's too costly. Expect that only 93 to 97 percent of the list is deliverable.

6. **If you want to "steal" a rented mail list, do it legitimately. Provide a free offer; when readers respond the names are yours.** Unauthorized reuse of someone else's mailing list is illegal and most lists are seeded to catch those who would do so.

If cold mailings produce results for you, continue. But also continue to test so that you do not find out that your mailing success is a fluke and short-lived. And if cold mail promotions don't work for you, shift to marketing techniques that have a proven track record as being more effective and efficient for professionals.

> When writing letters, increase their impact with a handwritten postscript. It will instantly grab the reader's attention and result in your letter being read first. And when preparing a sales letter, consider using a P.S. that does not clearly communicate, forcing the reader to go back and read the entire letter to grasp your meaning. For example: "Johnson accomplished this in 1976."

Q35

How profitable is it to follow up direct mail promotions to prospects with telemarketing?

Field research conclusively demonstrates that the pulling power of direct mail will increase with follow-up telemarketing. For example, a survey of 311 CEOs revealed that they often failed to respond to direct mail letters and brochures sent by professionals even though they found the offers of interest. They assumed that the professional would contact them again.

In another study of 446 professionals, it was found that telephone follow-up to potential clients who received a sales letter increased the opportunity to secure an appointment by 2.3 to 7.1 times. The average increase was more than three times. One accounting firm found that a personal telephone follow-up made by a partner increased by more than seven times the chance to secure an appointment to discuss the prospect's interest in retaining the firm. But it found that when clerical staff was assigned the task of follow-up telemarketing, scheduling appointments was only twice as great.

The most successful consultants have found that to make direct mail marketing cost-efficient and effective, they must limit the number of mailings to a level that permits timely and meaningful telemarketing by a professional staff member.

An engineering group with three professional staff members found that mailing 15 promotional packages a day (3,750 a year) was comfortable and productive. Each of the firm's three professionals was responsible for making five follow-up calls daily. Doing so generated an average of two appointments each week and 36 new clients annually.

One telecommunications consulting firm found the best results by establishing a strict schedule controlled by a master wall chart, as follows.

Day 1   Letter mailed
Day 6   Follow-up telephone call
Day 7+   Recall, if necessary
Day 10+ Schedule appointment

Q36
Should I write my own brochure or retain a professional to do so?

In most cases, you will develop a more productive brochure (capabilities statement) if you write it yourself. But the judicious use of outside assistance can produce even better results. Although you will find many marketing professionals interested in helping you avoid the daunting experience of developing a brochure, only a very few understand professional services marketing well enough to do a better job than you can do for yourself. And even those who are good at it need to expend significant time to understand your practice and the need of the clients you serve or would like to serve in the future. On the other hand, if you simply don't know where to begin or what to do, using an outside professional may be advisable. Perhaps it is best for you to do a first draft and then engage the services of an outside professional to review your work and make recommendations for change.

Developing a brochure takes some time and effort but really shouldn't be an intimidating or arduous experience. A good brochure describes what you have accomplished and outlines what you can do for the client. But its main aim is to get the potential client interested in you.

The place to start is to determine just what message is to be communicated to the readers. If the readers are diverse, it may be necessary to develop more than one message, more than one brochure. Consider writing a separate brochure (or capabilities statement) for each target market you serve. Concentrate on the benefits you provide to each particular type of client. General brochures (appropriate for everyone) are not usually sufficiently specific (relevant) to motivate the desired response.

The trick to deciding on the message to be communicated to the readers (prospective clients) is to ask yourself this question: What factors will result in the reader making his or her buying decision? Put another way, what are the determining buying factors? Your job is to write a piece that will cause the readers to come to think of you as the best of all possible sources to get the job done or make their problems go away.

Think hard about the message. If a one-on-one dialogue is essential to cause your prospect to retain your services, don't try to use your brochure to do what you must do in person. Clear and concise communication is important. You have but a few seconds to capture your reader's attention and interest. While research demonstrates that an interested prospect will read a great deal of information, a good brochure should raise as many questions as it answers. The purpose of such a marketing piece is to get the prospect to contact you, not to provide a reference work on your services, which removes the need for the prospect to obtain more information by talking with you.*

Carefully consider your communication style and medium. A brochure does not have to be written on an "8½ X 11" piece of paper. Do not fail to consider a brochure on a cassette tape, a filmstrip, videotape, etc. Most of us will still fall back on the written word but you may be able to make a splash, stand out, create a certain image through some less conventional means. If your voice is a strong ingredient in your sales appeal, put it to use.

----

*One management consulting firm developed a 28-page ("8½ X 11") capabilities statement. In addition to a few photos, it contained in excess of 18,000 words. It attempted to answer every conceivable question a prospective client might have. Although the firm mailed 20,000 copies to prospects along with a cover letter, they were dismayed to receive but a handful of responses and virtually no business. Follow-up interviews with some recipients caused them to conclude that few had the patience to read it. Those who did couldn't conceive of a question that had not been answered. Those who only skimmed felt embarrassed to call and ask questions; they thought that the answer to their question must be included in the voluminous text and thought that they should find time to complete reading the piece before initiating further communications.

Once you have established your prospective clients' determining buying factors and have decided on a medium for your brochure or capability statement, you must develop your message, decide what else to include, and begin designing your brochure.

Q37
What information should be included in a brochure or capabilities statement?

Since you must communicate to the readers in terms of those things that are important to them (determining buying factors), what you write or say is vital. Clients are far more interested in your accomplishments than in your credentials. The old adage that a Ph.D. and 10 cents (now, of course, 75 cents) will buy you a cup of coffee is quite true here. Research has demonstrated that the vast majority of clients want to know about the professional's accomplishments and contributions. Concentrate on past successes, not on your education, honors, and awards.

Write several descriptions (or vignettes) that will serve to communicate your track record and your ability to produce the kinds of accomplishments they envision when seeking your services. People new to private practice often are concerned that their lack of experience precludes their developing such vignettes. This is not true. Although successes and accomplishments may not have come from previous client assignments, they have produced reportable, tangible results. It is not really important to the potential client where the experience originated or how, if at all, the professional was compensated.

Selecting experiences you will include should be done with care. Don't necessarily pick your favorites. Ask yourself: Of all my accomplishments and successes, which are likely to be determining buying factors to my prospects? The following example of a vignette was included in the capabilities statement of a marketing consultant:

A major trunk airline desired to change its advertising campaign to spur a declining market share on its major (and highly competitive) routes. Traditionally they would periodically change promotional emphasis-from personnel, to timeliness, to food service, to quality of ground service, etc. The philosophy had been to keep the name of the carrier in front of the public and remind them of different benefits. Not fully satisfied with past successes, the airline and its advertising agency retained the Market Research Division of _____ and Company to find out just what the ads should say. In less than 60 days with an expenditure less than one week's media budget, _____ and Company undertook a comprehensive consumer study to determine those factors that caused a potential air traveler to select/decide on a given carrier in competitive markets. The results of this study were used by the carrier's agency to develop a totally revolutionary emphasis to the carrier's advertising program. Today, that airline is a leader in five of its seven competitive trunk routes.

The techniques applied in this important consumer research are applicable to a number of industries. We think you will be impressed by the innovative market research techniques utilized by _____ and Company.

In a very few words, the consultant has described and explained a substantial success. In addition, an opportunity has been extended for the reader to learn how such services might be of benefit.

In writing down your accomplishments, it is important that you stress the benefits gained by those who have made use of your services, and make it clear to the readers how they, too, can benefit from your services. Clients are not just looking for skills, they are looking for solutions and benefits, and that is what they must see in your capabilities statement.

In addition to vignettes describing your accomplishments, there are other types of information that you should consider including:

1. A list of previous clients or references. Do not link names of clients with specific accomplishments described in your vignettes because it will suggest that confidentiality is not a part of your services. However, a list of references or clients served is acceptable (with their permission, of course). Many professionals feel that it is not appropriate to place names of previous clients or references in the capabilities statement at all; however, you should be prepared to supply a list of individuals who can attest to your credibility, competence, and character.

2. Your credentials. Honors, awards, degrees, publications, professional designations, and the like, while not central to the decision to engage your services, add valuable reinforcement to your message. Be careful not to go overboard. While many of your credentials may be important to you, only a very select few will be of interest to your prospects. Don't underestimate the importance of practical, hands-on, on-the-job experience. For many clients it is a determining buying factor.

Be careful that your credentials don't intimidate. They should be presented almost as asides. Doing so will indicate that you expect to be retained on the basis of hard results you will produce, not honors received. For example, it might be better to soft-pedal your Ph.D. by subtly mentioning it in one of your vignettes. For example, "Methods developed while Ms. _____ was completing her Ph.D. (Stanford, 1979) were utilized in the development of _____."

3. A statement of your practice and operating philosophy. Describe how you run your practice, how fees are determined and charged; discuss your ethical principles, client-communication activities, etc. Ask yourself, "Is this information critical to the prospect's buying decision?"

Many professionals make the mistake of attempting to market the technical aspects of the services they provide. Clients are really interested only in the results achieved relative to their problems. A statistician found little demand for his services when he approached prospects asking if they needed his services. When he changed his approach to asking clients if they were interested in solving the queuing problem in their auditoriums, or the waiting line problem on their assembly line, he found interest. Clients didn't want to retain the services of a statistician; they wanted to solve problems.

4. The obvious but sometimes forgotten.   Remember to include your address, phone number, and other "obvious" but essential information that is too often accidentally left out.

Q38
Which should I do first—design my brochure or write the copy?

It depends on whether or not you are visually and graphically oriented. Some can't write the message they want to communicate unless they are able to visualize the layout and design that will convey the message. Others do better writing the copy first and allowing the message to guide design considerations. It may be best to prepare the design and the copy in tandem, making adjustments in each as appropriate.

Words on paper with a graphic design are not your only option. You should consider the use of other media such as audio or videotapes. The choice of media must be decided by referring to the market you are trying to reach. What media will your prospects find to be most persuasive and effective?

Assuming you, like most, choose to use the written word, what your capability statement says is important, but only if it gets read. The brochure should be designed with two important considerations in mind: (1) grabbing and holding the reader's attention, and (2) remembering that the design, format, and graphics say much about you to the reader—your prospect. The appropriate use of headlines and graphics can go a long way toward keeping the reader's attention. Moreover, the choice of typefaces, graphics, color, etc., has a significant impact on the way you are perceived. Unlike many other brochures, which are designed to be read once and then acted upon, a capabilities statement for a professional practice is usually designed to be read more than once and kept for future reference. Where other brochures might make use of garish colors and wild typefaces to attract the reader's attention, yours must be very carefully designed so that the appearance supports the message that you are a solid, dependable professional whose judgment is reliable. Yet it cannot be so conservative that prospects view you as less than vital, creative, or imaginative.

When you are preparing your brochure for production, you

may benefit by using professional assistance. Perhaps the best way to select a graphics consultant is to find out the names of the individuals who have designed brochures that you have seen and determined to be particularly effective and/or attractive. Be careful, however; your likes may be very different from those of your prospective clients. Photography, graphics, design, and printing are rather price-sensitive, so it is worth your trouble to shop for price as well as quality.

Having your capabilities statement designed by professionals is not inexpensive, but the results are often well worth the investment. To cut down or eliminate this expense you could learn how to do your own graphics and paste-up. A course in graphic design at your local community college will, over time, more than pay for itself in the savings you will realize by being able to use a T square to do some simple paste-up of copy and illustrations. And most large libraries have a number of books in which you can review the fundamentals of good graphic design. Even if you plan to use outside professionals regularly for this type of work, being aware of available options is useful. There are additional ways to produce professional-looking brochures at a fraction of the cost of buying them at street prices. For example, typewritten or word-processed material can be made to look (almost) typeset by preparing the copy with a distinctive typeface and justified right-hand margins, and then having it photographically reduced. Desktop publishing software is widely available at reasonable cost. However, in the production of brochures, it is also wise to aim high. This is not the place to save money by cutting quality. The few extra dollars you invest in graphic design, typesetting (by computer-based systems), paper, and high-quality printing will be more than repaid.

If you are developing a one-page ("8½ × 11"), two-sided brochure and are planning to print 2,000 copies, the difference in cost between a mediocre and a first-rate printing job may be only three or four cents per brochure. To realize the difference that a few dollars can make, simply remember the last brochure you received that was badly printed or on poor-quality paper and think about your reaction to it. The additional expenditure will be well worth the payoff in results.

One last thing to think about when it comes time to print your brochure: This piece of paper describes you and your practice. You are going to continue to grow and change as a professional, and your capabilities statement will need to change to reflect this. Avoid printing more copies than you need for the immediate future. You will want to change it long before you have the opportunity to distribute all the copies, and you will be reluctant to do so if you have several thousand in the storage room.

Q39
How can I get my brochure in the hands of viable prospects?

The best time to think about this question is before you write, design, and print your brochure capabilities statement. You should be market oriented. Determine the nature of the market and the message that causes the market to react in your favor. This analysis will usually affect both the wording and design of your brochure.

Distribution of the brochure can be done in a variety of ways. You can, of course, rent mailing lists and do a mass mailing. Such mailings, however, rarely produce a significant response, so you should test small mailings first.

Avoid pushing promotional materials on prospects and referral sources because doing so may give you the appearance of being needy and hungry for business. It is to your greater advantage to cause those who would benefit from such information to request it. For example, if participating in a panel or roundtable discussion at an association meeting (conference, convention, etc.), bury the inclination to place a copy of your capabilities statement or brochure in each participant's hand. Instead, when making remarks, describe the value of certain information that you have available and encourage those who would find it useful to give you a business card so that you may send it later. This avoids giving the impression that you are inappropriately anxious for business, while providing you the opportunity to follow up personally and specifically with every interested individual.

For the most part, you will probably find that your brochure is something you want to leave with a prospective client after a face-to-face meeting or to mail out after an initial communication in which the prospect has requested to know more about you.

It may also be effective to hand out brochures when making a speech or presentation to a business, civic, or professional group. Or brochures may be mailed out as a follow-up to those who attended and requested additional information. Give thought, too, to mailing a brochure along with a summary or transcription of your remarks and a letter indicating that there were so many requests for a text of your remarks that you thought you would send it to everyone.

Experiment, be creative, and continue to use strategies that work for you.

Q40
Do newspaper or magazine ads produce clients?

As inhibitions about advertising their services diminish, increasing numbers of professionals are experimenting with advertising, many with excellent results. Space ads can, indeed, be extremely effective devices for obtaining clients.

While you should probably not place all of your marketing emphasis on space advertising, it does have a valuable place in overall marketing strategy. Advertising in newspapers, consumer magazines, and trade and professional journals can supplement other means of direct marketing, such as direct mail, and support indirect marketing techniques (giving speeches and seminars, publishing, writing articles, etc.) designed to establish you as a recognized authority in your field.

Often professionals do better by not offering their services directly, but by identifying likely prospects for their services by offering some information item, such as a report, for free or at reasonable charge.

To create an effective advertisement, you must grab and hold the reader's attention. An ad can be innovatively and tastefully designed, impeccably laid out, and well-written but if it is not read and acted upon, it is useless. So seize the reader's attention and describe clearly the benefits of responding immediately to your ad. Do this by the following means:

1. Use the present tense and the second person ("you").
2. Appeal to the reader's senses. Give as physical a description as you can of the benefits of responding.
3. Use short, simple words in short, simple sentences.
4. Urge the reader to respond.
5. Provide clear and immediate benefit.

Be bold and straightforward, without reticence or self-effacement (even if you have a personal dislike for advertising), without hype or obvious overstatement.

Don't waste valuable advertising dollars by running business card or "tombstone" ads. They provide little motivation for the reader to take action.

Pay attention to how you read ads in a newspaper. Notice that strong, simple, and direct appeal is much more likely to make you stop scanning and actually read the ad.

Q41
Should my ad be general or highly specific?

The desire to get more bang for the buck motivates many professionals to create ads that will have the broadest appeal possible. They calculate as follows, "If I am going to spend all of these dollars to advertise, let me attract as many respondents as possible." This is a mistake. The more specific your ad and the more narrowly targeted, the larger the response.

While a general and nonspecific ad in a broadly circulated publication, such as *The Wall Street Journal,* or in a local daily newspaper may appeal to a wide range of readers and may persuade a few to call you, such an ad would have to run consistently over a long period of time to be effective. It will likely never be cost-efficient. Specific advertising will appeal to fewer people, but can rouse the interest of just enough of the right people—the real candidates for your services—to bring some business to your door. This ad:

RECEIVABLES FINANCED . . .
$100,000–$500,000.
3 Points Over Prime.
Accounts Over 90 Days Must Not Exceed 16%.
Any Industry.
Name, Address, Phone.

produced a response seven times as great as this ad:

FINANCIAL CONSULTING
No Assignment Too Small or Too Large.
Experience With Large and Small Clients.
Name, Address, Phone.

In addition, to achieve a cost-efficient and effective ad when your budget is limited, design an ad that produces an immediate, direct response. Advertising a free information item, or a no-charge initial phone consultation, for example, requires readers to contact you. Provide a response mechanism, such as a coupon, to facilitate quick replies. This kind of ad proves itself quickly, so that you need not spend time and money on unproductive repetition. Cash flow also may be improved because immediate-result ads usually produce revenue more quickly, reducing the amount of capital tied up in advertising.

Also, spend only enough money on space advertising to get the job done. Selling professional services almost always requires individualized, one-on-one selling; thus, most professional advertising is designed to create an inquiry, not a sale. Since professionals must talk with potential clients prior to gaining their business, they need not make a large investment in advertising to sell the service provided. It is usually much more efficient to expend small amounts to identify qualified leads.

In summary, to produce effective and cost-efficient advertising, be specific, target, seek immediate and direct responses, and spend no more than is necessary to accomplish the immediate job—making contact with your prospects.

Q42
How can I increase the pulling power of my advertising?

Most importantly, particularly when using small advertisements, your ad must attract attention and seize the reader. One way of making your ad stand out is using a sizeable amount of white space. But that's expensive. Well-written headlines can grab the reader's attention too.

Headlines should be short and punchy, promising the reader a quick, easy-to-understand benefit. Use words like NEW, NOW, HOW TO, ANNOUNCING, AT LAST, FREE. Using a specific date in the headline is often effective.

The slightest visual obstacle may prevent readers from finishing reading your ad. Thus, you should use the following to make your advertisement visually clear and compelling:

1. Short paragraphs.   Indent the first line of each paragraph. Use six lines or less, even if you have to break the formal rules of paragraph structure.

2. Ordinary, popular typefaces.   Use serif type, particularly if your audience generally is older than 35. Use sans serif type to make your ad look more contemporary, but only if your audience is likely under 35. Those with failing vision have more difficulty reading sans serif type if the size is small. Preferably, the type should be at least as large as that used in articles in the publication in which the ad is appearing.

3. Boldface words and phrases.   Impatient readers look at boldface first to get the gist of your ad.

4. Small pictures.   If you use pictures—of yourself, a product, a free offer—make sure they are of good quality, clear, and visually attractive. Use captions; picture captions are the best-read parts of most printed material. The captions need not explain the pictures. They should communicate your most motivating sales message.

5. Subheadings.   Plan them so that someone who reads nothing else gets enough information to respond to your ad.

6. Reply coupons.   A reply coupon is the surest way to bring about a decision. Ads with coupons are read more frequently.

7. Logos.   Even if your ad is not read, a distinctive logo increases your prestige and acceptability in readers' minds and the likelihood that your name will be remembered.

You want to avoid artistic effects such as white type on a black background—except for short headlines. Fancy special effects may make your ad hard to read, turning readers off and costing you potential clients.

Q43
How can I measure the results achieved by my advertising?

Since advertising is expensive, it is in your interest to measure carefully the results obtained. The best way to do this is to code responses. Ask respondents to write to a coded suite or box number or to telephone a coded extension. If you occupy Suite 506, you could direct response to Suite 506A for one ad, 506B for another, and so on. And respondents could be instructed to ask, when phoning, for extension 101 or 102. This will tell you exactly which ads are producing results.

Don't confuse leads with business. Some ads or advertising media may be great at generating leads, but may not produce qualified prospects that result in solid business. Others may attract fewer but more serious leads. Measure both leads and business obtained.

Don't hesitate to ask respondents to clip and send you the ad. An inducement for doing so (such as a copy of a booklet or report or even a sample copy of your practice newsletter with information of particular interest) will motivate such an action. This will not only tell you which ads are pulling, but it becomes the first step in "psychologically training" the prospect to take action and follow your direction.

You can, of course, use a similar system of codes for your

direct mail promotion and publicity campaigns. Doing so will tell you which mailing lists and which publicity efforts are producing desirable results.

Q44
How can I test the effectiveness of my marketing communications?

We are often the poorest judges of our work. Thus, when you write a sales letter, brochure, or advertisement designed to sell your services, always check it for readability. Either use a reading-level measure or give your writing to a 13-year-old child who reads on grade level and ask that child to tell you what you have said. You may be surprised to find that you communicate well above the level necessary to read the morning paper (approximately the reading level of a 13-year-old). You shouldn't. It will cost you clients.

In addition, every marketing communication should be tested to be sure that it communicates in the way intended. You can test the clarity of your communication by asking others to tell you what your words are saying; this is a test of face validity. Also important is the "test of image": You want to find out what assumptions, what feelings, others have about you as a result of what you have said.

One way to test face validity and image is to give your writing to at least three uninvolved people, asking them to tell you what your message says and what impression it gives about you or your firm. Do not give it to people who wouldn't want to hurt your feelings; they will not be frank. Give it to those who could care less about your feelings. If your brochure, advertisement, sales letter, etc., gives these people a significantly different impression of you, your firm, and your services than the one you want to convey, it's time to rework your promotion. Rework and reword until your marketing piece gives prospects the impression of you that you want them to have.

Another inexpensive and useful way to test your marketing and sales promotions is to contact the marketing department chairperson at a local university and explain that you would like to conduct some marketing research with one of the upper division or graduate marketing classes. The chairperson will probably refer you to a faculty member or the student marketing association and before long you will have a captured group to assist you.

This group should review your message (or perhaps a mock-up of your completed promotion piece) and in a simple test write down a description of the professional who would mail out this brochure, resulting in a sort of psychological profile. After you have collected the first written reactions, you can conduct a discussion with the group to get additional findings influenced by group process or pressure. Such a session will help you interpret their written response too. You will likely be very surprised by what you learn about yourself and your image. The information gained can be used to modify your communication and make it more effective. The changes you are contemplating will serve as a good ending for the class that has given its time. And the experience will provide them with a real-life lesson and allow the faculty member to explain the theory behind your research.

It might be a nice idea to make a donation to the student marketing association or the university library as a tangible expression of your gratitude. Doing so will probably help to make this resource available to you again. Everyone benefits from such a testing approach, especially you.

Q45
How can I test an ad or direct mail promotion inexpensively?

Careful testing is the only proven avenue to success in advertising or direct mail promotion. Successful advertisers follow a simple rule: test, test, test, and test some more. Testing gives you the feedback you need to develop effective promotions and to protect yourself against the whims of crazed inspiration.

If you are located in a major metropolitan area and elect to try newspaper advertising, test your ad in a smaller neighboring community before investing big dollars in the local daily paper. Your cost in a smaller community may be only 10 or 20 percent as great. Pick a community that resembles yours demographically and has a newspaper with about the same reader characteristics as the daily you will eventually use. You can exercise the same caution with radio, magazine, and direct mail campaigns. For example, send out

1,000 direct mail pieces, not 20,000. Such market testing enables you to determine whether it is worthwhile to spend money on the larger campaign.

For best results, you should test a number of different variables, among them:

1. Frequency with which the promotion appears
2. Dates and times when advertisement is run
3. Promotional message used
4. Size or length of promotion
5. Media in which advertisement is placed
6. Use of response coupon

With so many variables, if one attempt fails, it does not mean that the idea is bad; perhaps only one variable needs to be changed, or perhaps you just need a different combination of variables. Testing enables you to find out what works and what doesn't at minimal expense.

Keep track of the variables that affect the response to your ads. Placement on the page, the size of the ad, the headline, the absence or presence of a coupon—all can affect results. Record the response by ad and date so that you know how long it takes for the full response to come in. You might discover that for a daily paper, 60 percent of the ad's total response comes within two days after it is run, 20 percent on the third day, and 10 percent on the fourth; with this type of information, you can tell within a few days whether an ad is a winner or not. You can then make your advertising commitments accordingly.

If your early ads do not pull their own weight in immediate billings, don't abandon the whole concept of advertising. Experiment with different media, themes, free offers, graphics, and other factors. If you keep at it, you will learn which combinations produce results. Treat each less than totally successful ad as a valuable investment in knowledge. You can then build on your successes and avoid failures.

To achieve the most effective and successful direct marketing efforts, remember the following proven points:

1. The market is always changing.   What once worked is unlikely to work today. Expend effort to make marketing fresh and timely.

2. A given marketing communication will not be noticed by most prospects, at least the first two or three times.   Accordingly, repetitive marketing is productive. Marketing communications are only repetitious to you and a few who pay very close attention to what you are doing.

3. Prospects forget what you have said.   Repetition is valuable.

4. A given promotional approach is not motivating to everyone.   Using a variety of promotional messages that sell different benefits in different ways will increase response.

5. Sell benefits—that's what the market buys.   Most prospects don't buy technology; they buy the results of technology.

6. Give leadership and direction.   Many of the marketing campaigns that utilize the first five principles are unsuccessful because the marketer fails to tell the prospect how to respond, what to do, what action to take next.

5

DIRECT MAIL MARKETING: Selecting and Using Mailing Lists to Market Your Services

Knowledge of how to select and order mailing lists may be vital for the promotion of your services, and/or information products, whether you are planning to make use of indirect or direct marketing strategies.

Finding Mailing Lists

There are many places to obtain information about mailing lists, but the best place to start is with a copy of Standard Rate & Data's most valuable publication, *Direct Mail List Rates and Data.* Published every two months, *DMLR&D* is *the* source of information on mailing lists.*

DMLR&D lists in excess of 55,000 direct mail lists that can be rented (almost always for one-time use) or purchased (rarely). Examples of typical listings from *DMLR&D* will be found in Figure 5-1. Each issue runs over 1600 pages and is divided into classifications that enable you to locate the types of prospects that you are interested in reaching.

As good as *DMLR&D* is for identifying mailing lists, it is not complete. List authorities estimate that there are likely another 75,000 mailing lists available for rent that have not been listed in the directory. How do you find these?

One possibility is to talk to list brokers; they often know of lists that are available for rent but have not been listed in *DMLR&D*. Recognized mailing list brokers are listed in *DMLR&D*. But even talking to brokers isn't sufficient.

The little-known lists are usually only identifiable by effort— your effort in carefully analyzing the market to determine which individuals are most likely to be prospects for the services you are selling. While this will consume a significant amount of time, the effort will contribute meaningfully to your marketing success.

The best way to select responsive lists is to analyze the market by asking yourself, "What would my potential clients be doing, reading, joining, participating in?" Or, "What would be their identifiable characteristics in terms of income, education, location, lifestyle?"

By asking yourself these questions, you might determine that the best prospects for your services are members of some obscure professional or trade association that is not sufficiently market aggressive to have gone to the trouble of actively marketing their mailing list in any way. If, however, you contact that organization, they may well be interested in providing you with their mailing list.

---

*You can subscribe for $240 a year (contact SRDS at 3004 Glenview Road, Wilmette, IL 60091, phone 312/256-6067). You will also find the publication in any quality business library, particularly at major university schools of business and main offices of public library systems.

45 Business Executives

EDUTRENDS—cont

Rec'd Nov. 19, 1987.

4. QUANTITY AND RENTAL RATES

	Total Number	Price per/M
Total list (1986)	11,164	75.00
12 months	10,403	

Selections: ZIP Code, SCF, state; key coding, 1.00/M extra.

5. COMMISSION, CREDIT POLICY
20% commission to recognized brokers. Payments required within 30 days of mail date.

6. METHOD OF ADDRESSING
4-up Cheshire labels. Pressure sensitive labels, 6.00/M extra. Magnetic tape (9T 1600); 25.00 nonrefundable fee.

7. DELIVERY SCHEDULE
10 working days.

8. RESTRICTIONS
Sample mailing piece required for approval.

9. TEST ARRANGEMENT
Minimum 5,000.

11. MAINTENANCE
Updated quarterly.

ELECTRONIC BUSINESS MAGAZINE CIRCULATION LIST

Mid 025664-000

Cahners Direct Marketing, Cahners Publishing (a div. of Reed Publishing USA).
1350 E. Touhy Ave., Des Plaines, IL 60018. Phone 312-635-8800, Outside IL, 800-323-4958.
See listing under classification No. 95.

ELECTRONIC OFFICE EXCHANGE WANG BUYERS & INQUIRERS

(This is a paid duplicate of the listing under classification No. 236.)

Media Code 3 045 4746 6.00   Mid 033748-000

Electronic Office Exchange.

1. PERSONNEL
List Manager
J.F. Glaser, Inc., 999 Main St., Suite 103, Glen Ellyn, IL 60137. Phone 312-469-2075.

2. DESCRIPTION
Mail order buyers of and inquirers about factory reconditioned Wang word processors, small computers and related equipment.
Average unit of sale 3500.00.

3. LIST SOURCE
Direct mail and space ads in trade publications.

4. QUANTITY AND RENTAL RATES

Rec'd July 30, 1987.

	Total Number	Price per/M
Total list (0-12 months)	70,000	100.00

Selections: state, SCF, ZIP Code, 5.00/M extra; key coding, 1.00/M extra.
Minimum order 5,000.

5. COMMISSION, CREDIT POLICY
20% discount to recognized brokers; 15% to recognized agencies. Open account if credit is established.

6. METHOD OF ADDRESSING
4-up Cheshire. Pressure sensitive labels, 7.50/M extra. Magnetic tape (9T 1600 BPI); 25.00 fee billed if tape not returned in 30 days.

7. DELIVERY SCHEDULE
Allow three weeks.

8. RESTRICTIONS
Sample mailing piece required for approval.

9. TEST ARRANGEMENT
Nth name.

(D-B2, D-C)

ELECTRONIC PRODUCTS ACTIVE SUBSCRIBERS

Mid 025709-000

Hearst Business Communications, Inc.
645 Stewart Ave., Garden City, NY 11530. Phone 516-227-1300.
See listing under classification No. 95.

Elsevier Data Base

Mid 025421-000

Gordon Publications, Inc.
P.O. Box 1952, Dover, NJ 07801. Phone 201-361-9060.

1. PERSONNEL
List Manager—Val DeGaiso.
Broker and/or Authorized Agent
All recognized brokers.

2. DESCRIPTION
Unduplicated, merged list of recipients of 12 Gordon product news tabloids.
ZIP Coded in numerical sequence 100%.
Is computerized

	Total Number	Price per/M
Food tech. & service	1,997	
Textile & apparel	6,706	
Pulp & paper	10,438	
Lumber & woodwork	5,466	
Furniture & fixtures	3,782	
Chemicals (sub-total)	65,085	
Chemical processing	28,810	
Industrial	8,565	
Synthetic resin	3,889	
Pharmaceuticals	10,149	
Cleaning preparations	2,540	
Paints, varnishes, etc.	1,497	
Wood & gum	573	
Agriculture	1,376	
Glue explosives	7,686	
Petroleum	14,924	
Rubber	13,212	
Stone/clay/glass	7,831	
Biochemists	1,088	
Mfg. proc. end users	24,167	
Primary metals	19,819	
Fabricated metal products	74,475	
Retailers	61,762	
Machinery (except electrical)	75,598	
Electrical & electronic machinery	55,111	
Transportation equipment	14,078	
Instruments, photo equipment	11,028	
Misc. metal products	21,610	
Utilities	3,080	
Wholesale/distributor	21,17C	
Consultant	45,468	
Health services	13,16C	
Education	32,453	
Government	11,977	
Industry laboratory equip.	40,877	
Heating & plumbing manufacturers	2,828	
Industrial biomedical products	6,956	
Inhouse system int.	4,532	
Seminar	38,133	

Title:
Top management	221,518	
Middle management	247,575	
Mkt/sales	15,472	
Engineer	114,006	
Research & development	76,048	
Purchasing	29,519	
Professors	12,740	
Consultants	5,940	
Others	62,848	

Selections: state, SCF, 1 per company, 5.00/M extra; industry/title, 10.00/M extra; key coding, 1.00/M extra; each split of less than 5,000 names, 25.00 extra. Minimum order 5,000.

5. COMMISSION, CREDIT POLICY
20% commission to all recognized brokers; 15% to advertising agencies. Net 30 days.

6. METHOD OF ADDRESSING
4-up East-West Cheshire labels. Pressure sensitive labels, 7.50/M extra. Magnetic tape, 25.00 nonrefundable fee.

7. DELIVERY SCHEDULE
Within 5 working days. 24 hours if needed.

8. RESTRICTIONS
Sample mailing piece and letter of approval required. Publisher reserves right to refuse mailing. Re-use not allowed.

10. LETTER SHOP SERVICES
Available. Postage payable in advance.

11. MAINTENANCE
Cleaned and updated quarterly. Guaranteed 97% deliverable.

EMPLOYEE BENEFIT NEWS

Mid 043065-000

List Manager
Carnegie Marketing Associates, 20695 S. Western Ave., Suite 200, Torrance, CA 90501. Phone 213-212-0771
See listing under classification No. 169.

Enterprise Publishing Book Buyers

(This is a paid duplicate of the listing under classification No. 302.)

Media Code 3 045 4773 0.00   Mid 019155-000

Member: D.M.A.
Enterprise Publishing, Inc.
725 N. Market St., Wilmington, DE 19801. Phone 302-654-0110.

1. PERSONNEL
List Manager—Cynthia M. Scholes.
List Assistant—Suzan Paisley.

2. DESCRIPTION
Buyers of or inquiries about business related how-to offers on incorporating, tax shelters, raising capital, etc. Includes bookbuyers of How To Form A Corporation Without A Lawyer For Under 50.00 and The Complete Bank of Corporate Forms
ZIP Coded in numerical sequence 100%.

3. LIST SOURCE
Direct mail and space ads.

4. QUANTITY AND RENTAL RATES
Rec'd Jan. 15, 1988

---

5. COMMISSION, CREDIT POLICY
20% commission to all recognized brokers.

6. METHOD OF ADDRESSING
4-up Cheshire labels. Pressure sensitive labels, 7.00/M extra. Magnetic tape (9T 1600 BPI), 20.00 nonreturnable fee.

7. DELIVERY SCHEDULE
Two to three weeks.

8. RESTRICTIONS
Sample mailing piece required for approval. Mail date must be reserved. List owner must have option to rent mailer's list on a reciprocal basis. Cancellations beyond mail date charged full rate.

9. TEST ARRANGEMENT
Minimum 5,000. Nth name selection.

11. MAINTENANCE
Updated quarterly.

(D-B2, C-C5)

EXECUTIVE BUSINESS TRAVELERS

(This is a paid listing)

Media Code 3 045 4776 7.09   Mid 038221-000

Standard & Poor's Corp.

1. PERSONNEL
List Manager
Ed Burnett Consultants, Inc., 99 W. Sheffield Ave., Englewood, NJ 07631. Phone 201-871-1100. Toll free 800-223-7777.
All recognized brokers.

2. DESCRIPTION
Executives who travel frequently on business.
Selections available: state, SCF, SIC.

4. QUANTITY AND RENTAL RATES
Rec'd March, 1986.

	Total Number per/M	Price
Total list	260,000	60.00

Selections: sales volume, employee size, 5.00/M extra; phone numbers, 10.00/M extra; key code, 2.50/M extra.

6. METHOD OF ADDRESSING
4-up Cheshire labels. Pressure sensitive labels, 7.50/M extra; 3" x 5" cards, 25.00/M extra; sheet listing, 15.00/M extra. Magnetic tape, 20.00 nonrefundable fee.

(S)

EXECUTIVE BUSINESS TRAVELERS

Media Code 3 045 4780 5.00   Mid 043595-000

B & P Marketing Travel Consultants, Inc.

1. PERSONNEL
List Manager
JAMI Marketing Services, Inc., Two Executive Dr., Fort Lee, NJ 07024. Phone 201-461-9889.
All recognized brokers.

2. DESCRIPTION
Frequent airline travelers who have enrolled in one or more frequent flyer programs; 90% male.
ZIP Coded in numerical sequence 100%.

3. LIST SOURCE
Airline enrollment forms.

4. QUANTITY AND RENTAL RATES
Rec'd Jan. 18, 1988.

	Total Number	Price per/M
Total list	53,366	70.00
Business telephone numbers	32,000	+20.00
Home telephone numbers	32,000	+20.00

Selections: state, SCF, 3.00/M extra; ZIP Code, 6.00/M extra; keying, 2.00/M extra; telephone, 20.00/M extra. Minimum order 5,000.

5. COMMISSION, CREDIT POLICY
20% commission to all recognized brokers. Orders cancelled after mail date require payment in full.

6. METHOD OF ADDRESSING
4-up Cheshire labels. Pressure sensitive labels, 6.00/M extra. Magnetic tape (9T 1600), 25.00 nonrefundable fee.

8. RESTRICTIONS
Sample mailing piece required for approval.

EXECUTIVE COMMUNICATIONS

Media Code 3 045 4782 1.00   Mid 039119-000

Magna Communications.

1. PERSONNEL
List Manager
The Direct Media Group, Business List Management Division, 70 Riverdale Ave., P.O. Box 4565, Greenwich, CT 06830. Phone 203-531-1091.

2. DESCRIPTION
Subscribers and trials to a newsletter on audience involvement, sales techniques, use of visual aids, reviews of current speeches, dealing with the press, interpersonal communication, etc.
Average unit of sale 59.00 yearly.

3. LIST SOURCE
90% direct mail.

Figure 5-1   Sample listing from SRDS's *Direct Mail List Rates and Data.*

Perhaps it is available for immediate use as a mailing list, but often such obscure lists will require additional effort on your part to obtain mailing labels. Is it worth the effort of typing from index cards or a membership roster? Often it is if the list is particularly strong.

The more precisely you can identify the characteristics of your prospects, the better chance you have of reaching them and the better chance you have of finding a mailing list that is just right for your purposes.

Selecting the Best Lists from All Candidates Available

Your review of *DMLR&D* and other search efforts will likely produce a number of candidate lists that look promising. You must review the options and select those that have the greatest potential and that are in harmony with your budget. Don't turn over the responsibility for either list identification or final selection to brokers, advertising agencies or others. They may be extremely helpful to you in the identification and selection process, but no one understands your market and marketing objective as well as you. And, frankly, no one cares as much about your success as you. Get all the help you can but do not abdicate responsibility. Many direct marketing experts firmly believe that mailing list selection is the *most important factor* in the success of any direct mail marketing campaign.

Having already asked yourself questions about the nature of your prospects and which lists they are likely to be included on, you must again ask these questions relative to the specific candidate lists you have identified. In most cases, you will have identified more lists than you can afford to rent. Also, some of the lists may be extremely similar, if not identical, and you probably do not wish to mail to the same people twice. So, which lists do you select?

Going with intuition is not at all a bad idea; certain lists just seem to speak to you. Beyond this, however, consider price. Lists that are quite similar or even seemingly identical often rent for very different prices. There may be many reasons for the disparity in price, including the profit margin of the list owner. Often, more expensive lists are more expensive for good reason—they are better. List maintenance is not inexpensive. An owner who cleans a list often and engages in the necessary research to update and add fresh names will likely have to charge more than a competitor with a list that is old and needs updating.

But price alone is not a sufficient criterion for your decision-making. Talk to people who have used the list before and get the opinion of the broker. Here is where brokers can be most useful—they can tell you about the experience of their clients who have rented the list (and the competitive lists) in the past.

As a further consideration, look for guarantees. Many list owners guarantee the deliverability of their list. They may say that a particular list is 95 percent deliverable and agree to pay you for any "nixies" returned to them in excess of the guarantee. A higher guarantee often, but not always, denotes a better maintained and probably more productive list.

Evaluate the type of list! There are all kinds of lists. Among the more common are membership lists, buyer lists, subscriber lists, requests for information lists, and compiled lists. A compiled list is one that the owner has compiled from directories, address lists, etc. The nature of the list may greatly affect the quality of the list. If, for example, you are choosing between a list of *Fortune* magazine subscribers and a list of people who requested information from in-flight magazines on a commercial airliner, you will likely discover that the lists are of quite different responsiveness. Many direct mail authorities believe that the thin air associated with higher elevations combined with the free flow of alcohol almost mesmerizes otherwise serious people to "circle to death" all of those little numbers on the "bingo" cards in the back of the In-flight magazine. For some, such leads have proven to be of such small value that they refuse to even use the "bingo" numbers, contending that if individuals are not serious enough to fill out a coupon or call for information, they don't qualify as serious leads.

How Many Names to Rent and the Impact of That Decision on Selection and Profit

When you feel several lists have promise but your budget is limited, rent as many as you can afford. Particularly on a new marketing campaign or with a market test, rent different lists to determine which are most productive. Most list providers require that you rent a minimum of 3,000 or 5,000 names. When you want to rent only 1,000 names and request justification for their arbitrary policy, they tend to give you long-winded answers about their social responsibility in not allowing you to rent fewer names than is necessary to conduct a statistically valid test of the list. The real reason, of course, is that it is not economical for them to sell fewer than the arbitrary minimum. Some list providers have gone to $100 or $250 minimums rather than requiring that you rent a given number of names. Such externally imposed minimums should not be allowed to alter good decision-making on your part.

Sending out a direct mail promotion, using bulk mailing rates, will likely cost you around $350 per thousand units (35 cents a unit). You can spend less and you can certainly spend more, but $350 is a good average figure to keep in mind. If the cost of a mailing list is $66 per thousand (the current average) or 6.6 cents per unit, it may be in your interest to rent the 5,000 minimum required and mail the 500 or 1,000 you want to mail. What can you do with the rest? Save them and mail to them later if the first mailing produces results—or throw them away. Purchasing printing, postage, mailing service, etc., is far more expensive than discarding part of the mailing list. And the less costly the list rental rate—some lists are available for $30 and $40 per thousand names—the more relevant this approach.

In almost all cases, it is in your interest to rent several lists and mail a portion of each rather than to pin your hopes on just one or two full lists. Understanding why is very important to your success in direct mail marketing. Numerous variables can affect the response to a mailing: the headline, the copy, the market interest in the service being sold, the price, the terms and conditions of selling, the quality of the mailing list selected, and so on. By testing multiple mailing lists you may eliminate one of these variables—the mailing list itself.

Suppose you receive an inadequate response to your mailing. What's the cause? It could be any of the variables mentioned above or others. If you are mailing to several lists and one or two lists produce a high response, while other lists do not, you have learned something of great value that may well have a significant impact on your future decision-making. And, since lists are perhaps the most important factor in the success of a direct mail marketing campaign, it may be the most important lesson you could have learned in your initial test.

But don't forget another possibility. You are a great list selector; you select a list that does better than your highest expectations. On the basis of that result you nominate yourself for the position of direct mail authority of the year and roll out with a 100,000 mailing to capitalize quickly on the potential. However, perhaps that test mailing was a fluke, and the other lists are only marginally responsive. How are you going to pay the $30,000 promotion bill?

Testing is the key in direct mail marketing.

Saving for future use or even throwing away a few thousand names may be a small price to pay for the value of the information you gain by mailing to multiple lists.

The other important issue in deciding how many pieces to mail is the impact such a decision has on profitability. Some approach direct marketing with the idea of making a specific dollar profit. If this is your objective, your profit can be increased or decreased on the basis of the size of your mailing. The "Catch-22," obviously, is that the decision can also affect your loss.

A question almost always asked by mailers is, "How many pieces should we mail?" The answer is as follows: Suppose that you get zero response. No one buys. No one contracts with you for your services. How much can you afford to risk? Make the decision on number of units to mail in terms of how much of a loss you are willing to sustain.

This is really the only way to approach a test campaign. After some experience in the market, however, you will be able to determine what is called a "minimum response probability" and, thus, be able to make a more educated determination of the probable risk.

What about Duplicate Names?

If you are renting several different mailing lists, a given name may well appear on more than one list. People who subscribe to *The Wall Street Journal* are also quite likely to subscribe to *Business Week, Fortune, Inc., Forbes*, etc. Thus, a given person may receive two, three, four, or even more copies of your promotional piece. Those who understand direct mail marketing will know why. Others may feel that it's your error and believe that your organization is not cost-efficient or organized. Depending upon what you are marketing, this could have a negative consequence. To avoid such an image and to save dollars, many direct marketers don't order mailing labels, but order lists on magnetic tape. They then provide the magnetic tapes to their mailing house (letter shop) and have the mailing house do what is called a "merge/purge." Simply put, a merge/purge compares all of the lists, removes the obvious duplicates, and prints a new combined list.

It is important for you to remember that a merge/purge is very unlikely to remove all duplicates. Only the obvious duplicates will be removed. If someone has listed his name as "John Brown" on one mailing list and "J. W. Brown" on another mailing list, some merge/purge programs will not pick up this "human distinction." Moreover, the cost of a merge/purge is relatively high and unless you are doing mailings of at least 20,000 it may not be cost-effective.

Geography and the Size of Your Mailing

One way to control the size and cost of a mailing is to place a limit on the geographic scope of the mailing. Most mailing lists are available on the basis of zip code area and/or state. Your decision to limit the geography of the list you are renting should be based at least partially on the nature of the service being promoted. If you are selling computer software through the mail, geography is probably a minor issue. However, if you are selling seats in a seminar or professional services, distance from the buyer may be a very real issue. Experience suggests, for example, that a financial planner in Chicago will be more likely to secure viable prospects in the greater Illinois region than in New York, Atlanta, or San Francisco.

Ordering Lists

Identifying and selecting mailing lists (and dealing with the risk involved in the direct mailing business) is the hard part. Actually

PURCHASE ORDER FOR MAILING LIST RENTAL

[Letterhead]

To: _____   Date: _____ / _____ / _____

    _____   Number: _____

    _____   Ship Via: _____

    _____   _____

DATE LIST MUST BE RECEIVED: _____ / _____ / _____

SHIP TO ADDRESS ABOVE _____

SHIP TO _____   ___ Prepay charges and invoice

        _____   ___ Ship freight collect

        _____   ___ Estimated freight charges
                                               enclosed. Invoice for
                                               balance.

Provide on ___ Cheshire ___ Pressure Sensitive
           ___ Mag Tape ___ _____

___ Carbon copy of list ___ Merge/Purge ___ Key line (_____)

QUANTITY   LIST NAME/DESCRIPTION $/M   EXTENSION

_____   _____ $ _____ $ _____

_____   _____ $ _____ $ _____

_____   _____ $ _____ $ _____

_____   _____ $ _____ $ _____

        Total... $ _____

Method of payment: ___ Check enclosed   ___ Please invoice _____

Authorized signature: _____

Special instructions: _____

                      _____

Figure 5-2   Sample purchase order for mailing list rental.

ordering the list through the broker or directly from the owner/list manager is rather simple.

Figure 5-2 illustrates a form that you may use for ordering lists.

Mailing list brokers and advertising agencies earn a 20 percent commission on the rental fee (and sometimes on service charges such as selection fees) of list rentals that they procure for their clients. If you plan on renting a great number of mailing lists over time, it may be in your interest to establish your own list brokerage operation to save the commissions.

If you were to rent 300,000 names over the next twelve months at an average charge of $66 per thousand names, your total bill would be $19,800. The commission on such business would equal $3,960. If you are a broker, you keep that money. And well you should. You have done the work of the broker—which is not easy work.

6

SELLING PROFESSIONAL SERVICES:
Face-to-Face Methods for Marketing Your Practice

The first face-to-face meeting between the professional and the prospective client is the most crucial moment in marketing. What takes place in that first hour, how it takes place, what is said, and who says it, will determine whether or not you are successful in marketing and selling your services and will tend to establish the entire nature of the professional-client relationship.

Your marketing efforts result in the opportunity to meet with prospects. When you are actually face-to-face, you have moved beyond marketing to selling. Marketing is often difficult for professionals, but selling is even more so. Consultants often try to avoid marketing and selling because they feel that these necessary aspects of professional practice are beneath them or unprofessional. But every successful consultant soon learns that marketing (and selling) is essential. Your success is directly related to the development of a marketing and selling posture that is comfortable for you and your clients.

Marketing techniques employed should be very professional; they should instill confidence and enhance your image. Whether you accomplish your marketing through sophisticated public relations strategies, through direct techniques, or through a combination, it is marketing that will bring you to the attention of your potential clients and get you the appointment. Some professionals are sufficiently unique or prominent to have potential clients contact them. Other professionals must make the initial contact, either because prospects don't know how to make contact, are embarrassed about initiating it, feel uncertain, or simply pass up the opportunity. You, like most, will probably be doing some of both. If it's your move, you will find it necessary to take action that will attract attention—make you stand out and be noticed. You may even have to be a little "professionally" flamboyant. Getting an appointment requires that you convince prospects that it is to their advantage to have the opportunity to meet with you.

You have done the marketing, the preselling, and you have made the appointment; now you must be prepared for that first meeting. It is essential that you look at the professional-client relationship as one of peers. Some mistakenly approach the first meeting as though it were a meeting between superior and subordinate or as if it were a job interview.

In a job interview, you are seated in a low chair in front of a high desk. You are instructed to hand up things (like your résumé) for approval. It is a carefully calculated scene established to make sure that you recognize the relative importance and superiority of the employer and designed to ensure that you don't expect or ask for too much. But the first meeting with the client is neither a job interview nor does it involve a superior and a subordinate.

The first meeting is a meeting between peers, between professionals. You have as much right to reject clients as clients have to reject you. The purpose of the meeting is for both parties to determine whether or not it is mutually beneficial to work together.

You must take control of the meeting. Your clients will be looking to you to exercise leadership, direction, control, and authority. Even if this were your first client and your client's one thousandth professional, the client would be testing you to assess your managerial and directorial abilities.

Unfortunately—and understandably—many engaged in professional practice want to spend their time researching problems, assessing situations, and performing services. Consequently, they prefer not to concern themselves with "mundane" considerations such as contracts, payments, reports, and schedules, etc. They desire to provide the minimum management of client projects necessary to complete the job successfully.

Most clients, however, are management-oriented. They worry about contracts, invoices, payment dates, reports, etc. Unless you are directive and controlling with respect to such matters, your clients will quickly lose faith in you, despite your technical ability. Thus, your job in the first meeting is to sell your management skill as well as your technology.

You will find it advantageous not to look at this first meeting as a sales campaign. Rather, approach it as a professional meeting that allows you to make a decision based on the client's needs and problems and allows the client to decide whether or not you are the appropriate resource to handle those needs and problems. To that end, you must demonstrate your competence. You must convince potential clients that you, better than anyone, are capable of solving their problems, satisfying their needs, and diminishing their concerns. Only then will your services be retained.

But how do you demonstrate your abilities without giving away free samples? By talking about your experiences and the kinds of accomplishments you have produced for other clients. Don't reveal names or proprietary information; simply demonstrate that you are always around when these successes take place. Also, talk to clients in ways that cause them to feel that you are very intelligent, informed, strategic, creative, knowledgeable, but not necessarily by trying to solve their problems on the spot.

While you must demonstrate your professional competence, you also need to discover some information about your prospective clients, perhaps even before you say anything about yourself and your services. This strategy will give you some indication of the prospects' needs and problems and what they are looking for in a professional.

First, what has been their experience in using similar kinds of professionals: what did they like and dislike, what would they do the same or differently, what do they see as advantages and disadvantages of the professional-client relationship? Such information will give you a better indication of their feelings, attitudes, and impressions of working with professionals, allowing you to do a much more formidable job of selling your services to suit their needs and desires.

Second, you want to know on what basis clients worked with other professional practitioners. Did the contract call for a fixed-price, reimbursable costs, daily rate, hourly rate, cost-incentive fee, etc.? You don't want to know how much they paid previous professionals; that is none of your business. But you do want to know how they worked together because that helps you to determine the risk in the relationship: Either you are going to take the financial risk or the clients will assume the risk or you will share it. Understanding the parameters of the risk will help you establish how you and your clients will be working together if you elect to do business.

Third, do potential clients expect to pay for this first visit? Even though you may not plan to charge for this marketing and selling time, if prospects expect to pay (and about 15 to 20 percent do expect to pay for this meeting), they will also expect to receive highly specific and immediately useful information. However, you may be withholding such detailed information until some later time when you are in a position to charge a fee. As a result of miscommunication, your potential clients may view your lack of specificity as an indication of lack of ability and choose not to do business. Make sure to avoid such misunderstandings. Let your clients know up front what, if any, financial obligation they are under, and what circumstances or events give rise to financial obligation.

The fourth, and perhaps most important, question you must ask potential clients is what are the desired results of working together? What specific (observable) outcomes, results, changes, or differences must take place as a result of making use of your professional services to cause them to know that retaining your services was a wise decision? This information allows you to set fees, give estimates, establish time-lines or schedules for delivery of services, and level with clients about the reasonableness of their expectations with respect to the amount of resources capable of being committed.

Q46

How can I avoid appearing too anxious when I need the business?

The most successful professionals never appear to need business. No one wants to work with someone who appears to be needy or hungry. Thus, be sure you don't beg for business. For example, when setting a meeting time with a client or prospect, don't open your appointment book and say, "Anytime next week would be fine," because this gives the impression that you have nothing to do. Instead, say, "I am free to meet with you on Tuesday from 1:00 until 3:00 or on Friday between 9:00 and 11:00. Which would be best for you?"

Obtaining business requires that you communicate an air of indifference to prospective clients. Of course, this is hard to do when you need the business, but you will be more desirable to prospects when it appears (to them) that they need you more than you need them.*

---

*This is experiential, not intellectual. Intellectually, you can understand this concept, but it is very difficult to implement. You have to experience it. So practice. Select a group of prospects whose business you can live without. When marketing to them, practice being indifferent. For practice, try even discouraging them from making use of your services. Be aloof and indifferent. Communicate clearly that they need you far more than you need them. You will be amazed at the results. Doing this will teach you an important marketing strategy that you can tone and modify for future use.

The best way to be truly indifferent is to have viable options for how you will spend your time. Devote time each week to developing one or more proprietary projects or products—seminars, software, newsletters, manuals, etc.—that you can sell and that will produce equal or greater income than time spent providing services. Position yourself so that you can turn down undesirable, unprofitable business.

Such tactics not only give you workable options for your time but also help you determine the true value of your time and allow you to set the most appropriate fee to charge your clients.

Q47
Should I tell prospects about my past clients?

There are two important considerations. First is the ethical concern. If the client gives permission to release name and assignment information, you have solved the ethical problem, and if the client is a public agency, your services and the assignment are *usually* a matter of public record anyway.

The more important consideration, however, is how the disclosure of such information looks to the potential client. Does it suggest that some months down the road you will be using the client's name and problems in your marketing?

Experience suggests that you will be better off from a marketing point of view to provide your client with two distinct pieces of information: a list of clients and references (who have agreed to let you give out their names as references) and a separate description of accomplishments devoid of names. Then if the prospect wants to try playing the matching game, he may.

It may be best of all to tell your prospects something like this:

> It is my policy to avoid discussion of the particulars of my clients' business. The services I have provided for my clients are a confidential matter. I shall be pleased to discuss the nature and general character of the services I have provided—and, of course, I will be happy to provide you with references if you desire—but I am sure that you

will understand that I am unable to reveal the confidences my clients have entrusted to me.

The prospect, of course, fully understands and cannot help but admire your discretion. You also leave the prospect with the feeling that he or she can trust you and can provide the most proprietary and confidential data to you without concern.

Q48

How do I provide references if I'm new to private practice or am providing services in a new area of specialty?

Those new to professional practice and old hands expanding into a new area of service worry excessively about being unable to provide references. They fear that not being able to do so will cost them desirable business. They shouldn't!

Professionals do not get assignments because of their reference list. Indeed, if you find that you are frequently asked for references, something is wrong. You are likely not being sufficiently assertive, controlling, or directive. But no matter how assertive you are, a few will ask about your prior experience and request references. Even if you are new to private practice, you can supply references, and you do have relevant experience.

The potential client is not really too concerned with the fact that you have had no prior clients. You will not be retained because of a long client list. Clients are interested in your record of accomplishments. They are largely indifferent to whether your record was established as a result of serving prior clients, previous employment experience, or volunteer activities. Don't be concerned about being unable to give your prospects a long list of former clients. Your clients and the work you have accomplished for them is a confidential matter. It is sufficient to describe the nature of your experience; for whom the experiences were undertaken or achieved is confidential. If you talk about the business of former clients, potential clients will assume that before long you will be talking about them. However, this does not preclude you from providing prospective clients with a list of references. The list may contain the names of former clients, but there are certainly persons not your clients who can attest to your credibility, creativity, and character. Think of everyone you know: former employers, co-workers, professional and industry contacts, even friends.

Q49
How should I respond to a request for references?

Do not act surprised and flustered when the prospect asks you for references; you will look as though you lack credibility and experience. If you are asked frequently, you are not being sufficiently assertive. Remember this about references: You will likely be asked from time to time, but very few prospects will ever check you out. Why? You are asked because you have let the prospect get control of the situation. Not knowing what to say, the prospect makes small talk, which includes asking you for references. You won't be checked out, most often, because your prospects feel that you probably would not give as a reference anyone who would say anything unfavorable about you. You will be checked out, however, if you appear to be uncertain about how to respond to the request. The more important, well-known, and prestigious your references are, the less likely they will be contacted.*

One way of handling the request and putting yourself in a positive light is to carry in your briefcase, ready to hand out whenever appropriate, a list of references complete with addresses and phone numbers. When asked for your references, immediately and effortlessly extract the list from your case and provide it to the client, telling him to feel free to contact any of the individuals listed. The more names, within reason, the better; a list of about 18 people is better than a list of five. Before you cite anyone as a reference, make sure to ask for and receive permission. And remember that a reference need not be a past (or present) client; a reference can be

---

*One successful professional's reference list includes, among others, the President of the United States, two governors, United States senators, and several Fortune 500 CEOs. He's convinced that his prospective clients would be too intimidated to contact such notables, even though they are legitimate references.

any person who is able to speak for your credibility, integrity, skill, creativity, character, etc.

Q50
How can I prevent potential clients from pressing me to work for them full-time?

This is not at all an uncommon problem, and there are several strategies that will help to prevent your clients from attempting to convert you to their employee.

1. You must communicate to your potential clients the terms and conditions under which you are willing to make yourself available. Professionals are often vague in first meetings because they do not wish to run the risk of communicating anything that might scare off or upset prospects. Hence, they abdicate the roles of leader and director so vital to successful marketing of professional services. You must communicate firmly to clients that you are a private professional practitioner and are willing and able to provide your services only as such. Otherwise, they may see you as the valuable employee they have been seeking for years. Be sure to set the tone and direction of the meeting and relationship.

2. You must point out the benefits of retaining your services as an independent professional rather than as an employee. Frequently clients will be impressed with such factors as the cost savings that can accrue from the use of an independent, the value of not wasting your valuable time with typical organizational trivia and bureaucracy, the perspective and focus that comes from vast experience and external objectivity, and the fact that you have the ability to make the client organization self-sufficient and free from the need for continuing services. Other factors that might be pointed out include the growth opportunity for existing employees, lack of a long-term commitment that is typical of employment, freedom from the expense of fringe benefits, etc.

3. Clients should be motivated by the fact that in your role as an independent you have contact with many organizations and individuals that add both depth and breadth to your capability. You have a wider range of contacts and experiences, which enhances your value to clients.

4. As an independent rather than an employee you will probably be more objective. While objectivity may not be a major concern in all situations, it often is. You can provide impartiality and freedom of decision that most employees do not find to be in their interest.

Q51
How can I serve small clients unable to afford my fee?

Almost all professionals are contacted regularly by prospective clients with meaningful needs and potentially lucrative assignments but without adequate funds to pay for your services. For a variety of reasons they are unable to afford the professional's fees, and yet they are great people with whom it would be fun to work. Further, with the right help and financing, they could be very successful and you could profit by assisting them. Often, they propose (or they would be happy to hear you propose) that you serve them for a reduced fee, payments over (a long period of) time, in exchange for future profits, etc. How do you handle such requests?

When dealing with small, somewhat impoverished clients, you should consider charging a fee (even if small) for the initial consultation. This will serve to separate the serious from the time wasters.

Take great care to minimize the time you work with clients who want to compensate you on the basis of future riches. Either turn down such opportunities or limit the amount of time you are willing to invest in such ventures to a small proportion of your billable hours—perhaps 5 or 10 percent. In most cases, it will be in your interest to avoid working for a percentage of net profit. Instead, take a percentage of sales or gross profit. Net profit can evaporate quickly, but all enterprises that remain viable will have sales and gross profit.

Perhaps even better, find ways of serving such clients on a very cost-effective basis that will benefit them now while maintaining a demand for your services (at higher levels of compensation) later. Consider building a consortium of similar clients with similar needs, providing your services on a group basis, paid for collectively by the clients and affordable for all.

The opportunities for consortium research or services are common and frequent. You must identify a specific research or service activity that would be of interest to a group of clients. For example, one marketing consultant created a consortium of small ski resorts located in proximity to one another. None could afford his fees for marketing, much less the cost of media. But the seven resorts pooled their resources and advertised jointly. In another case, a grant writer built a consortium of several small, rural community colleges. By sharing the expense of his services, they found that they could have the services of a development office for which each had insufficient budgetary resources alone.

Good consortium research or services ideas have two main qualities: (1) the information researched or the services provided should not touch upon the proprietary interests or business strategy of your clients—not only are these areas confidential, but cooperative activity may be precluded by antitrust legislation; (2) the ideas should contain the seeds for an ongoing product or service. For example, a one-time report on consumer buying intentions might be rolled over into a quarterly update, perhaps even circulating beyond the original sponsors. To protect the clients' interests, you might publish generic data, keeping more specific information confidential. Both you and your clients will benefit.

Q52
How do I remain fresh and creative when selling a service I have sold many times?

If you have provided a particular service to clients twenty or thirty or more times in the past, doing it the next time is not going to be very different. However, all prospects or clients view their situation as unique. Granted, their situation may be just like everyone else's, but you will reduce their motivation to become clients (and your chances of selling your services) and look unprofessional if you are too pat, if you shoot from the hip, if you have ready answers to complex problems. They may need a Number 9, but you shouldn't communicate that that's what they are going to receive.

Thus, it is essential that you make sure you don't communicate such great familiarity with the prospects' problems or needs that you give the appearance that they will be getting a formula or packaged service. All prospects believe that their circumstances are unique and worthy of special, custom responses and solutions, and each deserves such individualized attention.

Make sure that you take the time and make the effort to examine and review every prospect's and client's situation from every possible angle so that you can offer a viable and very specific solution, tailored to specific needs and desires. With careful investigation, you may surprise yourself and find that a seemingly common problem is more complex than you would have thought. And even if you have handled such a problem hundreds of times, you must be like a professional actor giving the five hundredth performance. Only then will you get the business.

Q53
Does being controlling and assertive with clients always help?

In most cases, clients—even those very experienced in working with professionals—want to be directed and controlled (within limits) by the professional. Thus, clients will be seeking far more from you than your technical knowledge or capability; they will be seeking project management and procedural leadership.

Unsuccessful marketing efforts by professionals often result from "the problem of professional leadership." Most professionals prefer to expend effort on technical aspects of the assignment. Given the choice, they would rather not be bothered with managing. Consequently, they abdicate management, hoping that the client will take responsibility. If the professional fails to provide direction, guidance, and leadership on the procedural aspects of the project, the client begins to lose confidence in the professional's technical ability and will likely elect not to do business or further business.

This problem can be avoided by being appropriately assertive and controlling. In leading, don't forget to take responsibility for:

1. The circumstances or events that will determine the conclusion of the marketing phase and the start of the implementation phase of the consultation.

2. The terms and conditions of the contract, including such factors as who will prepare the contract, the time available for its review, and the date by which it will be signed.

3. The invoice schedule and the terms and conditions governing the time at which the client will make payment.

4. The services that will be charged for and the nature and types of expenses for which the client will be responsible.

5. The nature and frequency of reports to be provided to the client.

6. The terms and conditions, including notification times, that will govern termination of the agreement.

Q54

In the first meeting with a prospect, how do I get control of the encounter?

Gaining and maintaining control of the first meeting with a prospect is vital to securing clients. You must be thoroughly prepared and generally aware of all the client's needs. You must have the benefit of the client totally in mind and be prepared to explore all possible solutions to his problems. You will naturally and rightly be in control as you lead, direct, and show the way. And your prospective client will naturally follow.

Here are seven methods designed to assist you to gain control:

1. Make your first impression a good one. A strong and forceful (but not too forceful) greeting is a good start. Be firm and confident from handshake to opening statement. Dress is important too. Your dress and style should suggest command and authority without being intimidating.

2. Use your personality.   Don't be someone you are not! It won't work. Figure out your unique strengths and put them to work for you. Be comfortable with who you are. It has been said that the true sign of maturity is an acceptance of who and what you are.

3. Think positive . . . you are going to sell.   Have you ever gone to see a prospective client saying to yourself, "I hope to get a contract." Of course you have. We all have. But it's wrong. You will not succeed if you think in terms of hope, might, maybe, perhaps. These are negatives.

Always say to yourself, "I'm going to get this assignment. I can and I will get the contract because I've done my preparation and I'm convinced the client needs my service and I intend to sell him." Always think in terms of I can, I will, I must, I shall.

4. Exert control from the start.   Don't wait for your prospective client to tell you when you can start. Your confidence should exude from you so much (because of your thorough preparation and conviction that your solutions are best) that you will naturally make controlling statements and requests: "Could you sit over here, please?" "I will first demonstrate the outcomes that will be achieved, then I will show you how." Ask your prospect questions, start to give directions, keep control over your sales literature or examples . . . show them to the prospect when you are ready.

5. Give a smooth-flowing sales presentation.   Your prospect will tend not to interrupt if you have a consistent, effortless presentation. A smooth presentation reduces your need to exercise outward control. It will always be in your interest to maintain an aura of control.

6. Use a pattern of logical sequence.   The well-planned, logical, smoothly flowing presentation will help you in controlling the interview. A well-planned presentation answers all major questions and objections. It demonstrates that you are in control, in authority, and serves to reduce the objections and concerns of the prospect. Don't drag or meander. It will give your prospective client a chance to press and ask questions out of sequence. If this happens, you have lost control.

7. Speak forcefully and with confidence. When your behavior indicates that you know what you are doing, your prospect will perceive that and put confidence and trust in you. A weak voice or pussyfooting around will betray your lack of preparedness or belief in your own solution, and you will be in trouble.

Don't say, "I want to give you some information"; say, "I am going to . . . " Don't say, "I think"; say "I know." Don't say, "This might"; say, "This will."

It is up to you to take this candidate or prospect from the freezing point to boiling. If your prospect is bored or uninterested, it is your fault. When you do not earn the prospect's respect, you have lost control and lost a client.

Q55

How do I regain control in the initial meeting with a prospective client?

Far too many professionals create a communication vacuum in the first minutes of the initial face-to-face meeting and wind up losing control of the situation. Occasionally, it happens to the best and you must be prepared to regain control.

The prospective client who hears initial silence, slumps down in the chair across from you, and says, "Well, tell me about yourself," has just set the course for disaster. What do you talk about? What can you say to turn the prospect on to your services when you have yet to know what the prospect wants or needs? In such an open-ended void, simply say, "I'll be glad to tell you about myself. But first may I ask you a question?"

The prospect always says, "Yes." Then ask, "Can you describe for me the specific outcomes, benefits, and results you require (for the project under consideration)?" Once that question is answered, the next one is, "Can you tell me about the specific qualities you are looking for in engaging the services of an _____ (accountant, attorney, architect, engineer, consultant, etc.) to handle that assignment?" Take notes, either mentally or in writing, as the prospect answers the questions; you can then match your specific capabilities to his needs in response to the original question, should it ever arise again.

Asking such questions serves a dual purpose, allowing you to determine the prospect's needs and respond to them, thus improving your selling, and also letting you take subtle control of the meeting. It is essential for you to take control of the professional relationship, not to domineer but to exercise authority and convince prospects that you have the know-how and abilities to solve their problems and meet their needs.

Q56
How can I get prospects to recognize the value of my skills and experience?

Be sure that you translate your talents and skills into terms that are interesting and meaningful to your clients. People, including your clients and prospects, like to talk about what is interesting to them. Everyone likes to be the center of conversation; this fact often causes professionals to talk about themselves—my clients, my assignments, my interests, my skills. Such conversation is really not at all interesting to your clients. They want you to talk about them and their needs. Do not just waltz in on your client and expect to get the business by saying, "I'm a statistician. I am here to handle your needs for statistical analysis."

If you want to sell more and better professional services, it is your job to communicate your talents and skills meaningfully and intelligibly to your clients. That client probably doesn't even really know what a statistician does. What's more, the client may be unaware of how his or her needs or problems could be assisted by the work of a statistician. However, a client will respond if you explain exactly how your skills will solve X problem or reduce Y need and emphasize exactly what the beneficial results will be. Clients do not buy mechanics, procedures, and technology. Clients do buy results and solutions and benefits. Don't wow them with your technical jargon; tell them the bottom-line results you will produce.

Q57
How can I keep prospects from wasting my time?

Make sure that clients or prospects realize that your time is as valuable as theirs or even more valuable. People respect and do business on the terms proposed by those whom they regard as important and busy. For example, many are apologetic for taking up the time of a busy medical doctor, despite the fact that they are paying a high fee for the doctor's services. Alternatively, people often waste the time of a used-car salesperson because they don't think his time is of value.

In an initial meeting with a potential client who is wasting your time, try this: stand up and extend your hand. Thank the prospect for his time and say that you have a very busy schedule with many opportunities and commitments. Add that you would enjoy the opportunity to work with him and that he should feel free to call you when ready to do business (that is, serious, ready, and committed). Many professionals won't do this, afraid that it may cost them business. But, it will often be a highly effective way of getting business. Such an approach will cause the potential client to pay attention and realize that you are serious, busy, and committed. Your time is of such value that it can't be wasted by those unable to get down to business. If the prospect is interested in your services, he will contact you. Don't be surprised if he chases you down the hall and asks you to come back immediately.

Don't be a lapdog. Those professionals who are too available, too bending, rarely get the business. Do business on your terms and stick to your guns, but make sure that your business practices are professional and in line with the competition and with reasonable client expectation.

Q58
How can I ensure that marketing time isn't wasted by underlings not able to commit for my services?

A qualified prospect is one who has the need for your services, the money to pay for them, and the authority to retain you. Don't hesitate to insist that you meet directly with decision-makers. And before you start selling your services, prequalify prospects by asking them if they are in a position to make a commitment for your services if you can demonstrate a viable and cost-efficient method for meeting their needs, solving their problems, helping them take advantage of opportunities. Ask questions like these:

1. I understand that you have the responsibility for _____
   _____?

2. If I can demonstrate to you how _____
   can be achieved within your budget, are you in a position to commit your firm to retain my services?

3. Who, in addition to yourself, will participate in the decision to retain my services?

4. What is your budget to solve this problem?

5. What is your deadline for getting this problem solved?

Do not be embarrassed about asking these kinds of questions. Be self-assured, even forceful, and certainly businesslike. Your time, including your marketing time, is very valuable. Spend it wisely by qualifying your prospects before seeing them.

Be careful not to run the risk of angering subordinates or making their lives difficult. The boss may have instructed them to gather information or do the legwork. It may be wise to suggest that you would find it desirable to have both them and the key decision-maker involved in the initial meeting. But establish and communicate a philosophy that your time is of great value and that you must spend those valuable and limited hours meeting with those who have the authority to engage your services. You want to make it clear, without being perceived as arrogant, that kings meet with kings, prime ministers with prime ministers, and undersecretaries with undersecretaries, and that you clearly are a king.

Q59

What are some good questions to ask to quickly get a handle on the client's needs?

The ideal client is prepared when first meeting with you. Problems or needs have been identified and, in some cases, the underlying causes isolated. Perhaps solution approaches have been developed internally. In such circumstances, you may have to confirm the client's assessment of need, but your role has been pretty well prescribed. More commonly, the client has given inadequate thought to problems, needs, causes, and available solution strategies. Your first task is to figure out the problem and then recommend an approach. While this makes your task more difficult, remember that if clients took time to do the careful analysis required, you might not be retained. Perhaps as much as one-third of the demand for your services arises as a result of the fact that clients are too busy to take the time to do adequate internal preplanning and analysis. You are retained because it is easier to delegate the problem than to think about it.

The needs-analysis stage of your work can be lengthy and complex. In such cases, it may be best for you to contract to do a formal needs analysis or feasibility study. The results of this effort (for which you will be compensated) will include a proposal to solve the problem. If the client finds your analysis acceptable and your proposed solution appropriate, your services will likely be utilized further.

During your initial meeting with the prospective client, it is useful to have a number of questions to ask that will help you translate the client's vague dissatisfactions and concerns into specific needs (areas to be analyzed in a more formal needs analysis). To guide you to develop questions appropriate for your selling situation, consider this list of questions developed by an accountant/ business consultant:

1. What is the major problem that this organization faces?
2. What problems do you face that are shared by the rest of the industry (or similar firms or agencies)?
3. What problems confront your organization that are unique to this geographic area?
4. In what ways has inadequate planning contributed to the problems facing your organization?
5. In what ways have government regulations affected the profitability of your organization?
6. How does this organization rank in terms of salary, benefits, and employee perks with others in the industry?

7. Is this organization family owned? If so, to what extent does this ownership affect promotions and employee morale?

8. What kind of staff turnover have you experienced? Is this trend up or down from previous years?

9. Based on your assessments of employee satisfaction and productivity, what changes in personnel policy seem indicated?

10. How long have your key management and technical people been with your organization?

11. How far in advance do you make specific decisions about expansion?

12. What is the most disappointing area of growth that was not realized over the past two years?

13. In what ways do you ensure that expenditures on training will produce the desired results?

14. How do communications work within your organization?

15. How do you identify communications breakdowns in the organization?

16. Who reports to whom in your organization?

17. What is the biggest time bomb in your organization? What steps have been taken, or do you plan to take, to deal with this problem?

18. What impact do you see the pending proxy fight having on management and staff?

19. What new products or services do you see as vital within the next ten years for this organization to maintain or increase the growth rate that has been experienced over the past three years?

20. How do you plan to deal with the capital crunch expected in the next two years?

When communicating with prospects, avoid asking questions to which you already know the answer. It makes you seem dull and uninteresting, as you probably will not pay much attention to your prospects' answers. Do not waste their time. If you have nothing new, creative, and interesting to say or ask, you probably should not be talking to them in the first place.

Don't hesitate to take notes. Reliance on memory can be dangerous and clients will be flattered that you find their words of sufficient significance that you want to make a record of them. Questions such as the ones above, and others that you develop, can help you assess the needs and desires of your prospects and clients in order to tailor your services and offer the best and most productive solutions to their problems.

Q60
What questions, even if not asked, should I be sure to answer when selling my services?

When meeting with potential clients, be sure to answer the five questions that prospects need to have answered but frequently fail to ask:

1. How will I profit from your advice or services?
2. Why will I profit from working with you?
3. How can you demonstrate that I will profit?
4. To what extent will I profit from your advice?
5. When will these profits or benefits be realized?

You should also anticipate some of the following questions that your prospects will have in mind—even if they do not ask them—when deciding whether or not to retain your services.

- Do I need this service?
- Do I really want this service?
- Can I really afford this service?
- Will I make use of the outcomes?
- Am I being given a good deal?
- Should I check out the competition?
- Could I get this service for less?

o Is this professional honest, knowledgeable, and reliable?

o Should I decide now or later?

o What will my colleagues think?

o What adversity will result if I don't act or don't act now?

When you respond honestly, intelligently, and persuasively to these unasked questions, your prospects will be favorably impressed with your intuitiveness and keen perception of what is on their minds. Learning and using such strategies, asking perceptive questions, and laying fears to rest should help you turn uncertain prospects into solid clients.

Q61
What are the principal fears a client is likely to have about retaining my services?

Research with more than 600 clients reveals the following fears, in priority order.

1. Fear that the professional is incompetent.   Many are concerned that the advisor talks persuasively but may not have the know-how necessary to accomplish the objective.

2. Fear that the professional is incapable of being properly managed or directed by personnel in the client organization.   Some prospects perceive professionals as competent but too controlling, too self-directed, and are afraid that they will lose control of the project and/or lose authority to control the situation or outcome.

3. Fear that the professional has insufficient time available to complete the assignment on schedule.   Some are afraid that the professional will be unable to devote adequate time or provide the necessary resources to complete all tasks properly in a timely manner. Some professionals add to this fear during marketing by trying to impress the prospect with how busy they are and how important their client list is.

4. Fear that the fee charged is too high.   Many clients are concerned that they may be paying too much for the proposed services, despite the need for and value of the services.

5. Fear that the need for the services of an outside professional is an expression of the client's own failures or limitations.   In some fields, it is fashionable to use independent professionals; in others, needing such assistance is viewed as an admission that the client organization may be performing inadequately.

6. Fear of disclosure of sensitive proprietary data.   There is serious concern that the advisor will not be totally discreet with the information obtained as a result of interaction with the client organization.

7. Fear that the client has not properly diagnosed the problem.   Interestingly, many clients are more concerned with their own inadequate diagnosis of their problem than with that of the professional. These clients are afraid that their incorrect or incomplete information will cause the professional to expend expensive time in needs confirmation or analysis rather than in responding to the needs identified.

8. Fear that the professional will not be impartial.   There are two issues of concern here. The obvious one is that the professional will have some priority other than the client's interest, or some conflict of interest, that will color objectivity. True professionals never allow their evaluations and decisions to be governed by any objective other than the client's best interests. But even the most ethical, disciplined professionals are prone to see the solution to all problems in terms of more services; this tendency is so pervasive that a professional can recommend unnecessary add-ons without being aware of this bias.

9. Fear of developing a continuing dependency for the professional's services.   Some prospects are afraid that they will have a continuing need for the professional's unique services and will never become independent.

Many of these fears can be alleviated. If you are highly visible and recognized as an authority in your field, you increase the chances that prospective clients will respect and trust you. Moreover, providing impeccable references will further enhance your prospects' impressions of the desirability of retaining your services.

And you should develop the skill of being able to identify during the first meeting which of these fears are a priority for your prospects. Then you are able to respond to individual concerns. Make sure you demonstrate your knowledge, skills, and experience to rule out the fear of incompetency. Be assertive and in control but not so much so that prospects fear that they will lose authority; explain what managerial role they will play in projects. Convince potential clients that no interest comes before that of the client, and that they will be your top priority. Make sure that you have no conflict of interest and emphasize your discretion (take care to avoid discussing the particulars of previous client assignments). Justify your fees and ensure that clients know exactly what will take place in exchange for the fee paid. Also, communicate schedules or time-lines for projects.

Do not think that a denial of prospects' concerns is all that is necessary to sell your services; however, laying such fears to rest and gaining trust and respect, are essential to professional selling.

Q62

Will telling my client the blunt truth ever hurt my business?

As a professional, you have an obligation to be blunt, frank, and totally honest with your clients. They sometimes need to hear bad news, even if it winds up costing you future business.

Most professionals realize that it is good and necessary to be tough with the client with respect to how the consultation will be conducted, what the fee will be, and when payments will be made. But another kind of toughness is required, too—being tough on advice. Tell your clients what is wrong and why. Do not couch your criticism in such nicely worded, third-person recommendations that the client can misinterpret. Tell it like it is. Some clients need to be hit over the head to wake them up and bring them to a recognition of reality.

You know this, of course. So why do so many professionals avoid being frank, honest, and blunt with clients? They are afraid of upsetting clients; they are fearful that they will lose business. So they pussyfoot around and their advice winds up being regarded as perhaps "good" but not "essential."

Unless you are seen as "essential," you have no security. You are a bad investment because you don't do your job. The very first business turndown and you are gone. That is what being nice does to you. What does it do for your client? Nothing.

So be honest, straightforward, blunt, but don't embarrass clients in front of others. Your reputation will grow and new business will result. Of course, being honest will cause the loss of some clients. But, do you really want the business of such clients?

Q63
What face-to-face selling strategies have professionals found most effective?

There are two primary stages in the process of turning a prospect into a paying client: the marketing stage and the selling stage. Marketing and selling are quite different and, thus, require different approaches and strategies. Through your marketing strategies, the prospect should be convinced of your credibility, integrity, and the quality of your services. Marketing prepares the client to be sold by setting the expectations for doing business with you. However, when you are face to face with your prospective client for the first time, marketing professional services stops and selling professional services begins. Once you have reached the selling stage, you must know your prospect's needs and desires and be prepared to respond to them. You must also have determined and be ready to address the ideas, attitudes, and feelings that will motivate the prospect to retain your services.

Many professionals try to be efficient in selling. Since they would prefer to spend time on client projects and assignments, rather than on getting the business, they adopt a canned approach for getting the business. Doing so is unproductive and can be detrimental to marketing and sales efforts. To be successful, you must develop and adopt selling strategies comfortable for both you and your prospects. The following techniques can help enhance your selling and make it more effective:

1. Improve your face-to-face selling abilities by observing and responding meaningfully to the individual image and style of your prospects.   By being observant—to body language, dress, office furnishings and art, time management style, pace of communication, attitudes, feelings, etc.—you will learn to individualize your selling techniques and treat prospects and clients the way they want to be treated, without ever being anything less than yourself. This obviously isn't as efficient as you might desire, but it is effective!

2. Within reason, dress the way your prospects or clients dress.   Don't be overly formal or informal; if you don't know how your prospects dress, err on the side of being more formal than informal. Dress is an important facet of overall style and can affect the way in which your prospective clients perceive you.

3. When selling your services, don't talk too much.   You should be speaking 40 percent of the time or less. One way to check yourself is to record a few of your presentations to make sure you aren't spending too much time talking and too little time listening.

4. Don't oversell.   Keep clients happy by spelling out exactly what you will accomplish, the probability that your efforts will achieve the desired result, and the risks associated with the services you will provide.

5. When following up on a proposal or sales call, don't call and ask if the prospect is ready to give you the business.   Doing so gives the impression that you are hungry and needy. Instead, find a tangible reason to communicate with the prospect: new information; an important, relevant, or interesting event with which he or she may not be familiar; etc., and use that as a rationale for your call.

6. Be sure to communicate what action you want the prospect to take.   Whether selling your services by letter, in a phone call, or in person, don't fail to spell out precisely the next step for your potential client.

7. Engage in trial closes—a selling technique used by all successful salespeople. Throughout the meeting, successful sales people ask simple questions or make small comments designed to test how well they are communicating their message. Good salespeople don't say, "Would you like to buy this?" They say, "Would it be more convenient if we deliver it on Thursday or Friday?" They assume that the prospect has decided to buy. When the prospect says, "Well, I would prefer a Friday delivery," they have given a buying signal. You don't say, "Would you like to retain my services?" Instead, say, "When we get started, my experience suggests that it is advantageous for us to make a joint presentation to the branch managers. Would next Wednesday be a good time to do that?" When you operate on the philosophy that the decision has been made—that it is so obvious you are going to be retained that you need not even ask the question—you get your potential client thinking in those terms, too. In fact, after discussing all the subtleties and options of the assignment, it becomes almost embarrassing for the prospect to say, "Well, I'm not sure I want to do it." By this point, if the prospect is a good candidate for your services (and the prospect should be a good candidate if you have reached this point in the selling stage), he will be sure of the wisdom, value, and benefits of making use of your services.

Q64
What strategies work best when selling my services to a committee or board?

Many professionals find it difficult enough to convince one decision-maker of the advisability of engaging their services; when the solo decision-maker is replaced by a committee or board of directors, the task of selling becomes seemingly impossible. But it's not that difficult. The key to success in selling the "multi-headed" prospect is to take time to talk to each individual who will be involved in the decision to find out their specific agendas and concerns. Pre-sell each in terms of their considerations, and when meeting with the committee as a whole demonstrate how you are providing adequate balance to ensure that individual concerns are met. This is clearly more time-consuming than just meeting with one party, but properly executed it makes your selling job easier. You can establish allies on the committee who will endorse the wisdom of doing business with you.

In addition, if a governing board is responsible for making a decision to do business with you, be sure to try to obtain an invitation to attend the board meeting at which your services and contract will be discussed and decided on. If it's a public agency, no problem—board meetings are open to the public. If not, you might tell the executive administrator, "I would love to see what goes on in that board meeting and observe you handling the board. In my experience, boards are more motivated to contract when they see that the 'vendor' is sufficiently interested to attend the meeting. If a highly technical question arises, I would be available to you as a resource. I have found that it's a good strategy when starting your presentation on this contract to let the board know I am in the room and point me out."

At the meeting, you will be introduced and members of the board will want to talk directly to you rather than to the executive administrator. They get to talk to the executive every week; you're new. Thus, you will end up in control of the meeting, will essentially make the presentation, and in doing so be able to use the selling strategies that you know will have the greatest appeal.

Q65
How do I evaluate the effectiveness of my face-to-face selling skills?

The number of prospects whom you turn into solid clients is a good indication of how good your selling skills and presentations are. However, other factors also contribute to turning a prospect into a client. The following checklist may help you evaluate your sales presentations. Rate yourself 1 to 5 (with 5 being high) on each of the following criteria of a good sales presentation:

1. I always ask several strong qualifying questions of the prospect to find out what the problem is or what compelling benefits are desired.   ☐1 ☐2 ☐3 ☐4 ☐5

2. I enhance the prospect's confidence by always presenting several ideas that will satisfy his problem or needs.
☐1 ☐2 ☐3 ☐4 ☐5

3. I let my prospect know that what I offer is a unique service and that no one else can provide the advantages I make available. □1 □2 □3 □4 □5

4. I always prequalify or requalify and seek commitment by asking questions such as, "If I demonstrate to you that I can overcome this problem for you, will you be able and willing to retain my services?" □1 □2 □3 □4 □5

5. I explain all the features of my proposition and take care to emphasize the benefits of greatest importance to my prospect. □1 □2 □3 □4 □5

6. Every sales presentation I make includes several comparisons between what the prospect has now and what I can provide. □1 □2 □3 □4 □5

7. When possible and appropriate, I utilize simple and clear graphs, slides, pictures, or other illustrations to provide visual as well as auditory stimulus in my sales presentation. □1 □2 □3 □4 □5

8. I provide my prospect with illustrative success stories of how others have benefited from adopting the proposal that I offer, but avoid disclosing confidences. □1 □2 □3 □4 □5

9. Every time I make an important sales point, I get my prospect to agree that this is something he wants. □1 □2 □3 □4 □5

10. Throughout my presentation I get my prospect to make many "yes" answers so as to condition the prospect to say "yes" to me. □1 □2 □3 □4 □5

11. I anticipate the objections or fears my prospect will likely raise or have, raising them myself and responding to them before he has a chance to bring them up. □1 □2 □3 □4 □5

12. I take great pains to prove to my prospect that I don't mind answering questions on any point I make. □1 □2 □3 □4 □5

13. I always introduce the testimonials and endorsements of people that the prospect will respect. □1 □2 □3 □4 □5

Add up your scores and enter the total. If your score is 52–65, you are probably doing a great job in making sales presentations; 40–51, you could probably revise that sales presentation and do a much better job; 0–39, your sales presentation is probably quite poor and you should consider extensive revisions. This brief checklist is not the absolute test of your ability to sell your services; however, it can point out some of your strengths and weaknesses.

Q66
How can I avoid giving away valuable services for free?

There are four primary situations in which it is likely that a professional will give away services for free unless precautions are taken.

1. Whether selling your services face to face, by telephone, in a letter, or with a formal proposal, don't specify how you will achieve the desired results in such detail that you enable the client to achieve the result without your involvement. A less detailed or specific proposal will not result in lost business. In fact, your client really does not want to hear about your technology; instead, the client wants to hear about the benefits of retaining your services. Thus, you need to develop in-depth proposals that concentrate on the results of the project and not on procedures.

2. Professionals often give away free advice after seemingly having finished an assignment. In such a situation, the professional accomplishes the objectives, provides the results, and ends the assignment; however, the client encounters some implementation problems and seeks further advice or hands-on assistance. If this happens once or twice, it is probably quite reasonable for the professional to help without charging an additional fee. But when the requests for aid and assistance become habitual, action must be taken. In such cases, either an invoice should be sent to the client for the additional services, or the professional and client should enter into a new agreement—perhaps a time or availability retainer. Explain both options and let the client specify a preference.

3. When prospects cannot identify their problems or needs, the professional should propose undertaking a diagnostic evaluation for a specified fee. Such a project usually includes developing a proposal that not only identifies the problems or needs,

but also specifies a particular action plan. However, there are times when you begin to think that no matter how accurate your diagnosis is, the client is not going to retain your services, and you will end up giving away valuable time (and service) diagnosing the problem without compensation. In such situations, you can refuse the project and walk away without performing a diagnostic evaluation; however, there is still the chance that the prospective client might provide some real business. Your best option is to suggest working under a diagnostic contract that compensates you for the analysis and the action plan you propose. If the client chooses not to retain you to implement your proposal, you have already been compensated for your time and services. If the client retains you, you might deduct the charge for the diagnosis from the total fee for the project.

4. When a professional is under contract to perform an activity, the client sometimes suggests, "As long as you're doing this, why don't you handle that too." When this occurs, you may be unsure of the client's commitment to the extra work or his plans to pay you for it. The best approach is to agree to perform the extra work, making sure to inform the client that any change in the scope of work produces a change in the budget or estimate. The client can then decide if the increased expenditure for the additional work will be beneficial, and you can be certain that you will be compensated for any added services.

Q67
How should I handle requests for free services from friends, relatives, or colleagues?

Every professional has a certain number of friends, relatives, colleagues, and associates who attempt to obtain advice for free or at a substantial discount. In all fairness, some don't even realize that they are taking advantage. People who are not engaged in professional service themselves often fail to realize how valuable time is for a professional.

The key to not allowing such requests to become a burden on

your time or to make you "friendless" in short order is to anticipate such requests and respond instantly in a way that lets the requesters know they are taking advantage.

There is nothing wrong with saying, "That's not an easy question. To do what you want to accomplish would take a considerable amount of time and analysis. If you are really serious, I would be happy to provide you with an estimate or a proposal."

One professional faced such constant requests that she decided to put all likely requesters on notice, by sending the following letter.

Dear _____:

I am writing to inform you that effective _____, my firm, _____, has established a new service—THE ADVISORY.

Because so many people desire my advice on a time-to-time basis, THE ADVISORY is designed to serve my clients, friends, and associates in a new way previously not possible. Different from the formal contracts I usually work under, THE ADVISORY is intended to make easy the opportunity to have a question answered, or a quick review of an idea, concept, or piece of work.

THE ADVISORY will not require a proposal in advance of services to be performed or a formal contract that specifies services to be performed. THE ADVISORY is available at any time without prior arrangement and is activated by the phone call or question. Services provided will be invoiced at the end of the month.

Sincerely,

Exercise restraint in turning clients into social friends. The close working relationship and shared interests often encourage doing so, but it can hurt the professionalism with which services are delivered and have a negative impact on the clients' willingness to refer business. Many professionals find it desirable to establish a firm policy of not doing business with friends.

Once she put people on notice, she felt free to answer their questions and charge accordingly. There is nothing wrong with answering an occasional question, but when such questions begin to take up your valuable time without providing any compensation, it is time to protect yourself. All but the most dense will get your message.

Q68
Should I exchange services with other professionals?

Exchanging services is usually frustrating and disappointing because one party always perceives that he or she is getting the advantage. But the advantage quickly deteriorates when the obligations and responsibilities surface. For this reason, exchanges should usually be avoided. Even though it seems that both parties will benefit at the start, one is likely to wind up feeling disappointed, frustrated, taken advantage of, or otherwise unhappy. In many cases, both will feel that way. Why? There are several reasons—and any one of them may be sufficient grounds for your establishing a policy of no exchanges, except in the most unusual circumstances. The following vignette serves to illustrate the disadvantages and drawbacks of exchanging services.

George desires the software package sold by Anne but would prefer to avoid paying the $1,500 in hard cash that Anne charges. Thus, he proposes an exchange of services; he will design a promotional brochure for Anne in return for the desired software plus custom installation and programming. This exchange has several failings:

1. The services provided by George have a lesser value to Anne than the services she will be exchanging. Had Anne desired the brochure as much as George desired the software, she would have already contracted to have the work done by George or another professional.

2. Because of Anne's perception, she will be a more demanding client. To get what she perceives to be "fair full value" she will be more picky and difficult to please than most.

3.   To make the deal, George will be less open in explaining the limitations on the services he is willing to provide and may even (somewhat unintentionally) lead Anne to believe that she can expect more than he would normally deliver at such a price or fee.

4.   As Anne becomes more demanding, George will begin to evaluate the parameters of the original understanding. He will increase his perception of Anne's "profit margin" and become increasingly aggravated about her expectations.

5.   One way George will compensate for his feelings that the deal is a "little raw" is to place Anne's work in a lower priority. And because of the pressures of "cash paying clients," he will keep moving her job further down the list.

6.   When Anne begins to complain about George's tardiness, George will in turn find it to his advantage to become picky about Anne's work. He will now become the complainer, asking her to make adjustments and do extra work, trying to create guilt. His hope is that Anne will come to view his less than professional behavior as being caused by her less than professional work.

7.   Both are likely to wind up having a less than favorable impression of the other. They are not likely to do business together again. Nor should they expect referrals from one another.

They will both come to ask: "Was it worth it?" And in most cases, they are likely to conclude that they would have been far better off to do business for dollars, not services. George would probably have spent far less time and effort—and certainly suffered less stress—if he had expended his time finding a client willing to pay $1,500 or more for a brochure. The fee received would be adequate to fund the purchase and installation of the software. And Anne would likely have been time and money ahead if she had expended her efforts in obtaining just one client to fund the investment in a brochure—if that was really what she wanted.

Q69
How do I deal with efforts by the client's staff to torpedo my success?

When working with the client's staff, you may be perceived as a threat. The potential for incompatibility between you and the staff may cause the client to resist retaining you, continuing to use your services, or providing follow-on business. Although it is not possible to overcome fully the threat an independent professional creates, you can reduce it and make it more acceptable by doing several things. First, make sure that your client introduces you properly to the staff and explains your role. This includes your being positioned as a supporter and not an adversary. Second, reduce the threat by communicating the fact that you plan to work through the staff and not at their expense. To convince the client that your relationship with staff will enhance the consultation, not hinder it, and to improve your working relationship with the staff, practice the following:

1. Be informative. Explain the purpose and benefits of your request to the staff yourself. Even if they should know, they may not.

2. Be cordial. They are not your subordinates. You need to concentrate on subtle influence and the use of informal power. Don't expect to get results with authority and control.

3. Take time to listen. They may have ideas that are different from yours and their superiors'. Gain their cooperation by

---

Don't allow your relationship with the client to deteriorate into one that is adversarial in nature. Your role is to serve the client's interests. Keep communications open and honest. If communications deteriorate, stop providing services and patch up the professional-client relationship before continuing.

listening to what they have to say and understanding the motivations behind their thoughts.

4. Work through them.   You may be perceived as a threat to their position or status in the organization. Convince them, with words and actions, that you are there to make them look good.

Q70
Will turning down business hurt my image?

You can enhance your professional image and credibility by recommending that your services not be used for certain needs a prospective or existing client may have. When prospects or clients can do something for themselves or when there are other professionals or commercial organizations that can provide certain services more efficiently or effectively than you, let them know. In addition, avoid undertaking any assignment for which you are not fully technically competent or lack the resources necessary for producing the desired accomplishment.

Improve the cost benefit for your clients by asking yourself each month (or week) for every client: What am I doing for them that they could do for themselves? You may discover many services that the client does not (any longer) need you to provide or perform. Point these out to the client and suggest a strategy to help the client become self-reliant. You will have happier clients and they will tell others about your professionalism, which could lead to more referral work and additional follow-on assignments.

Be willing to admit mistakes and errors and bring any bad news to the attention of your client promptly and professionally. You are only human and it is inevitable that from time to time you will make errors or be in a position of having to be the source of bad news. Handling these difficulties in a professional fashion furthers your professional image and stimulates referrals, particularly with the more sophisticated client.

Even if you need the income and/or the business, never accept business from clients who you feel don't really value your services, who might ask you to do anything unethical or questionable, or with whom you have personality conflicts. In the same vein, never refer another professional whom you do not trust and respect completely to clients or to anyone else. One of the surest ways to hurt your own referral opportunities is to be seen as a person whose judgment is less than entirely appropriate and reliable. If the people seeking referrals keep pressing, you can always provide the names of two or three individuals that you understand may provide the desired service but of whose abilities and ethics you have no first-hand knowledge or experience. Be sure to remind them that these names come with no endorsement and that they will have to satisfy themselves with respect to their suitability.

Avoid making any disparaging remarks about the competition or past clients. Doing so suggests unprofessional behavior and will hurt business and referrals. Explain why your services are better and the unique advantages you offer. If you really are better than the competition, it will be obvious to your clients and prospects. And there are always ways of communicating caution to clients about other professionals and to colleagues about prospects or clients by saying little or nothing or with the creative use of intonation.

Being scrupulously professional in all your dealings with prospects, clients, colleagues, and your competition will enhance your image and reputation, increasing your business and success.

Q71

What are some simple, low-cost ways to stimulate additional business from existing clients?

The best prospects for your services are existing clients. Devote a minimum of 30 minutes a week (uncompensated) for each significant client, figuring out what additional ways you could be of benefit to them, and document your information in the form of a mini-proposal such as a letter or memo.

Spend half a day, at least twice a year, walking around the reference room of a major university library. Examine interesting books, directories, and guides. You will discover many innovative marketing opportunities and new services that you could provide to your clients. Keep abreast of news and anything else pertinent to your clients; read a major-market/high-quality daily newspaper

and several business, trade or professional, and consumer magazines regularly. Be aware of changes, trends, and events that affect
and influence your clients.

Consider tape recording short consultations or phone conversations with your clients (with their knowledge and permission)
and providing them with a copy. It makes your services even more
beneficial because your clients wind up with tangible evidence of
your work together, one which they can refer to after the project
has ended.

In addition, turn wasted TV or air travel time into productive
marketing. Photocopy an item of interest to prospective and existing clients and use this time to write them a personal note and mail
it to them. Handwrite your note and envelope, and use a stamp, not
a meter, for maximum benefit. These people will think about you;
will appreciate your perceptiveness and thoughtfulness in taking
the time to notice, photocopy, and send the news; and will, in
many cases, provide additional business or referrals.

Find creative ways to remind clients of the impact of your
accomplishments. When writing letters, memos, and reports, or
making presentations to client staff, refer (unobtrusively and
quickly) to past successes. But don't overplay your role. Sometimes
you will be more successful if you bury your ego and let key players
in the client organization get recognition for your achievements.
It's often tough to do, but it's good for business. Those who are
really important to future business and referrals will know that you
are responsible for the accomplishments.

Schedule a series of meetings (perhaps four to six a year) and
invite good clients and prospects to attend without charge. Give
each meeting a theme, such as "How to Increase Your Collections
with the Telephone" or "New Technology in the 1990s—How It
Will Affect Your Profits." Bring these people together, under your
leadership, to discuss the issue. Your clients will appreciate the
chance to meet (for free) with you and their colleagues and
exchange valuable ideas and information, and you will have a
chance to show your knowledge and expertise and help to identify
new needs of those attending.

Survey past and current clients to assess their needs and the value of your service (fee they are willing to pay), and use information to define new services that you should be providing.

Uncompensated time and effort on behalf of clients pay off in additional business and referrals.

Q72
How can I make myself indispensable to clients?

In addition to providing quality services:

1. Accept the difficult collateral or side assignments. Take responsibility for accomplishing small tasks and projects (not directly related to your primary mission) that staff or other professionals are trying to avoid.
2. Send short, informative memos to clients advising them of additional opportunities or problems you have identified.
3. Take time to train client staff members to be self-sufficient and not dependent upon you to do the task.
4. Stage decisions for the client; quantify risk factors, costs, and benefits whenever possible.
5. Arrange choices and alternatives in order of priority in terms of the client's values, but avoid usurping the client's right to make decisions.

People are reluctant to refer business (or engage in business directly) when they feel that the referred party will experience a long-term, expensive involvement with the professional who is benefiting from the referral. Increase the potential for referrals, business, and your perceived benefit by taking care to communicate that one of your operating philosophies is to train the client and client's staff to be self-sufficient and free from the need to continue obtaining the desired results through outside professionals.

6. Inform clients regularly on problems experienced and expected in connection with the timely and successful completion of your work.

However, of all of these strategies, the best way to make your clients dependent on you is to make them self-sufficient so that they can grow and expand, providing you with more significant opportunities and challenges.

Q73
How can I obtain publicity for successful accomplishments for clients?

In some cases, you will find that the press has an interest in the accomplishments you produce for your clients. If the client views such publicity as beneficial, you might work jointly to bring your results to the attention of the media. Consider, too, the possibility of getting meaningful mileage out of a final report through publication. Would your client be interested in having you write a final report in the form of an article for a trade magazine or journal? Although you will probably do all the writing, you will find it beneficial to share authorship. Such an article could be written in case study style: problem, alternatives, solution approach adopted, outcomes.

The public relations and marketing benefits for picking up future clients and building reputation and professional image are obvious. Not so obvious is the fact that the participating author/client gets attention from the article, perhaps serving to motivate follow-on assignments. In addition, recognizing the problem and taking steps to correct it is good public relations for the client's company (particularly within the financial community).

Always be viewed by your clients and other prospective referral sources as giving at least 110 percent. You benefit when others perceive that you provide more and better services than they bargained for and than others in the business.

7

PRACTICE MANAGEMENT: The Marketing Implications

Many professionals tend to fear, dislike, or dismiss the business or managerial aspects of professional practice as much as they do marketing and selling. However, setting and disclosing fees, and writing proposals, contracts, and reports are essential elements of marketing and selling your services. They will show the client the importance you place on each project and the effort you expend on every detail of providing services. Realistic fees suggest that you are confident of your abilities, respect the value of the client's dollars, and provide quality services. Proposals focusing on benefits and tailored to the client's needs reflect your understanding of the client's problems and desires. And straightforward, concise contracts as protective—or more—of the client as they are of the professional show that you value the client's interests and the client-professional relationship and desire to make your services productive and beneficial for all concerned.

The time to begin thinking about your fee is not the moment that a prospect asks, "How much will this cost?" A realistic fee schedule should be established at the time you commence practice and should be modified regularly. Your fee is based on your skills and expertise and the client's need and demand for your services. It should be calculated by establishing your daily labor rate (the value of your time) and adding overhead (the expense of being in business) and profit (the return for the risk you take by being in practice—normally a percentage of the total of daily labor rate plus overhead). While the scope of work for a project can be adjusted to fit a client's resources and requirements, there should be no reason to negotiate your fee if it is reasonable and calculated fairly. It is best to be open about your fees, making it clear to clients that state-of-the-art services and expertise require fair market price. Research demonstrates that the fee charged plays a very minor role in the decision to retain your services. Indeed, fewer than one-third of all clients talk to two or more professionals before deciding to engage your services; fewer yet obtain an alternative bid or estimate.

For many professionals the proposal plays a major role in marketing and selling—in the prospective client's decision. The proposal must persuade the client of the tangible benefits of retaining services. It should detail the results to be achieved, without outlining methods and procedures so specifically that your services are no longer needed. Often the proposal is the last selling effort, and a well-written, persuasive document (or verbal presentation) can make the difference between gaining or losing a client.

Contracts, progress reports, and final reports serve to reinforce the marketing and selling that has taken place and to enhance the professional-client relationship. The written agreement or contract, in particular, is essential to clarify the working relationship, spell out the terms and conditions of the project, and avoid misunderstandings. Progress and final reports enhance communication with the client (and others directly or indirectly involved); they help to track progress, identify problems and achievements, and facilitate evaluation of the overall efforts.

Skill in executing these aspects of professional practice—set-

ting and disclosing fees, writing proposals, contracts, and reports—
and in discussing them with clients will improve your marketing
and selling success markedly and enable the client-professional
relationship to function smoothly.

Q74
How should my services be priced?

Consultants need to price (pure) professional services, customized
products (services capable of being quickly and easily modified and
resold), and pure information products (software, manuals, seminars, newsletters, etc.). The strategies used to price each are quite
different.

 Professional Services: The majority of professionals price their
services on a cost plus basis. They determine hourly or daily rates
or fixed-price or fixed-fee contracts by first calculating costs (professional labor and overhead expense) and then adding a profit percentage. Such a calculation might be as follows:

6 days × daily labor rate of $400	= $2,400
Overhead (90 % of labor rate)	= 2,160
	$4,560
Profit of 25%	= 1,140
Total Fixed Fee	= $5,700
Daily rate ($5,700 divided by 6) = $950	

Increasingly, professionals regard this approach as simply a means
of establishing a fee or price floor. The amount actually charged a
client may be significantly higher, based on client need or market
demand. Thus, if the above services have a greater value to the client, perhaps of $7,500, the professional might charge more than
$5,700. If the client is unable or unwilling to pay $5,700, the professional should turn down the assignment (a lower fee is below
the floor) or cut the scope of services to justify a lower fee.

 Customized Products: Many professionals use their creativity
and talents to develop services that are capable of being modified
and remarketed to other clients. Lawyers, for example, must invest
time up front to develop a trust agreement. Once created, it can

serve the needs of many future clients with only modest modifica-
tions. How should such replicable services (customized products) be
priced? Some professionals attempt to collect the full development
cost from each client. Doing so creates a handsome profit, but in
the long run can serve to make the professional noncompetitive. It
is more appropriate to amortize the total development costs over
the expected number of replications. For example, suppose you
determine that an investment of 150 hours of professional time will
enable you to create a highly effective strategic planning training
program. Further, you calculate that with an additional investment
of 20 hours the program can be refined to make it very specific to
the precise needs of a given client. And, you assume that over the
next three years the program will be able to be sold to 20 different
clients. You might price as follows:

Initial Development:
150 hours × hourly labor rate of $60	=	$ 9,000
Overhead (106% of labor rate)	=	9,540
		$18,540
Profit (20%)	=	3,708
		$22,248
Cost of capital, 3 years	=	2,781
Total Development:		$25,029

Per client development cost:
$25,029 divided by 20 = $1,251.45.

For each client you should add $1,251.45 in development costs to
the other costs incurred for such things as customization and program delivery or conduct.

Pure Products: When creating pure information products,
price should be established as it is for any product. You must determine the answer to this question: At what price will maximum profits be generated? Price testing, of course, is the best way to get a
handle on this question, and different price strategies are available,
including skimming the market first. The total development cost is
amortized over the life of the product.

If you are pricing a manual, cassette series, specialty publication, etc., which will be marketed through direct mail, don't set the price on the basis of what you find at the local bookstore. Specialty publications can and do command a much higher price than mass market offerings because they have a more limited market, shorter production runs, more expensive distribution and marketing costs.

A book on planning may sell for $29.95 at a trade book outlet; however, a book on planning for hospitals (which likely won't even be sold at the local bookseller) will probably command $40 to $60. If the book is for an even more limited market, perhaps planning for the hospital critical care unit, it will likely sell for $60 to $90.

Professionals balk at paying high prices for mass market merchandise as much as anyone, but they anticipate higher prices for information products that are specifically directed toward and pertinent to their field, specialty, needs, and purposes.

Q75
Is it better to work for a fixed price or for a daily or hourly rate?

Slightly more than 44 percent of all professional service contracts are completed under terms by which the professional is compensated for actual time expended plus direct expense. Most of these professionals have established either a daily or hourly billing rate, or both. These billing rates include salary, overhead expenses, and profit. An additional 33 percent of professional service contracts are completed under terms of a fixed price (or fixed-fee-plus-expenses) agreement by which the professional establishes a fixed price that includes salary, overhead, direct expenses, and profits for which he or she will be compensated.

Some situations preclude a fee based upon a fixed-price contract. Those consultations for which the advisor is unable to estimate with accuracy the labor involved and/or the direct expenses to be incurred should not be done on a fixed-price basis. When labor can be accurately estimated but direct expenses cannot, it is best to work fixed fee plus expenses.

One advantage of the fixed-price contract is that most clients prefer to pay for services on a fixed and certain basis rather than on a time and materials basis because a fixed price eliminates a great deal of risk on their part. They prefer to pay a set fee without having to worry about how much time or expense the project requires. Moreover, clients are used to paying for things on a fixed-price basis; almost everything we buy in our daily lives has a fixed price.

Yet many professionals prefer to work on an hourly or daily rate. Why? It eliminates the requirement that the professional take risk. If estimates are in error, the client will merely pay for more (or less) time and actual direct expenses. With the fixed-price contract, of course, it is the professional who takes the risk.

Is the fixed-price contract or the daily (hourly) rate more profitable? Research indicates that despite the additional risk the professional assumes in working fixed price, the benefit of doing so can be substantial.

Looking just at profits of some 76 professionals, with whom in-depth follow-up analysis was conducted, it was found that profits of those working exclusively on a fixed-price basis were 87 percent higher than those working exclusively on a daily (hourly) rate basis.

When profits and professional salary were added together, it was found that the fixed-price group had profits and salary that were 95 percent greater than their daily (hourly) rate colleagues.

For those utilizing both daily (hourly) rates and fixed-price contracts, it was found that profits were 32 percent higher and profits and salary 36 percent higher than those billing clients exclusively on a daily (hourly) rate basis.

It is interesting to note that of the practitioners working exclusively on a fixed-price contract, costs exceeded estimates in only 24 percent of the assignments. Among those working both fixed price and daily (hourly) rate, actual costs exceeded the estimate used for determination of the fixed price in only 12 percent of the assignments for which a fixed-price basis was utilized. This would seem to reflect that assignments that were more difficult to estimate were undertaken on a daily (hourly) rate basis.

When asked if these situations of cost overrun were a function of poor estimating or poor "project/assignment" management, more than 73 percent of the exclusively fixed-price group (and 59 percent of the fixed and daily/hourly rate group) reported that poor estimating was the cause.

This certainly reflects the need for assistance in improving the ability to estimate.

This assumption seems particularly reasonable when you consider how professionals working exclusively on a fixed-price basis evaluated themselves regarding their ability in estimating. Of those who ranked themselves as very good at estimating, costs exceeding original estimates were evident in only 14 percent of the cases. Of those who evaluated themselves as being not very good in estimating, the percentage was 29.

Thus, while the fixed-price contract may be more profitable than the daily rate fee, and more acceptable to clients, it is not going to be profitable for the professional unless he or she can estimate accurately. The key to profitability in fixed-price contracts is reliable estimates. If you learn to make sharp estimates, the fixed-price fee can be very lucrative.*

Q76
Is working on a retainer advantageous?

A retainer is a contractual method of providing services that makes the professional available to the client for a specified amount of time or scope of work. A good retainer is one that is predictable. If you have no idea at the start of the month whether you will be spending five hours or five days with the client, you have a bad retainer.

With a *time retainer*, you receive a set and predetermined dollar amount each period (for example, each month) for a predictable level of effort or service, such as analyzing client financial statements or making recommendations for management action.

A *base retainer* should be used if you are unable to determine in advance the amount of service the client will require. For example, you agree to provide out-placement advisory services to all terminated managers and executives of the client. Since there is no sure way to know how many will be terminated, you cannot agree

---

*More information in greater detail can be found in *The Contract and Fee-setting Guide for Consultants & Professionals* (John Wiley & Sons, 1990) by Howard L. Shenson, CMC

to a set dollar amount of compensation. You might, therefore, agree that you will spend up to three days a month on this activity in exchange for a fee of $2,500. Further, you agree to charge for time spent in excess of the three days at a specified figure, perhaps $1,000 a day. The client pays for the three days whether or not they are used.

With an *availability retainer*, the client is guaranteed that you will be available, if needed, for a specified amount of time, perhaps two days a month. In exchange, you receive a sum usually equal to 25 to 30 percent of the value of your time. If your daily rate is $750, you might receive $400 per month just to be available. If your services are used, you either receive your normal fee of $750 a day, plus $400, or just the $750, depending upon the wording in your agreement.

Sometimes you will hear the term *advance retainer*, or *front-end retainer*, used. This is not really a type of contractual agreement, but a term to indicate that the client provides funds in advance of your providing services. Services provided are invoiced against the advance.

In all retainer agreements, be careful to keep the retainer period reasonably short. Many professionals think that they want a long retainer—of a year or two. This is likely not in their interest. What they really want is a short retainer that is renewed over a long period of time. Here's why:

Implicit in the word "retainer" is the notion that once the retainer period has expired, the agreement to provide the services has terminated—even though the fee remains a client obligation. Suppose you have an annual retainer to provide 24 days of services in exchange for $1,500 a month. Both you and the client assumed at the time you agreed to work together that the services would be delivered in two-day increments monthly.

Should the client fail to request services or provide data necessary for you to do your work, your obligation has not expired. In theory, the client could come to you during the last month of the retainer year and request that you deliver all twenty-four days of contracted services. If, however, you had agreed to a monthly retainer that would be renewable for or continue on for a year, the two days contracted for would expire each and every month. Thus, in most cases, it is in your interest to have short retainers that last for a long period of time.

A retainer can be either advantageous or disadvantageous depending on the type of contractual agreement you prefer, the type of services you provide, and the scope of services to be performed for the client. It is certainly to your benefit to study the issue carefully and perhaps to seek legal counsel when considering the use of a retainer.

Q77

What's the best way to obtain a start-up payment or front-end retainer from a new client? What percentage of the fee can be obtained prior to delivery of services?

The decision to request a start-up payment or front-end retainer from a client should be based on several factors, including the size of the contract, the nature of the client, and the length of time from start of the assignment to completion. The willingness of a client to agree to such a request is a function of additional factors, such as the professional's negotiating skill, as well as the motivation of the client to obtain the services being provided.

If an assignment is to be completed on a fixed-price or fixed-fee basis and the duration of the project is several weeks or longer, obtaining a start-up payment is more acceptable. Generally speaking, the longer the duration of the assignment the lower the start-up payment as a percentage. For example, one marketing consultant found little problem obtaining a start-up payment of 20 percent ($6,200) on a project involving a fee of $31,000 where the work would be completed over a seven-month period. The same consultant received a start-up payment equal to one-third of the fee on a six-week project with a fee of $15,000. One-third of the total fee was paid at the start, one-third at the end of the third week, and the balance on completion.

Front-end retainers and start-up payments are well advised and are quite acceptable to most clients. For the professional, such payments improve cash flow and may serve as a protection to ensure that payment for services provided is received. Such payments are even appropriate for hourly and daily fees. One management consultant has established a firm policy: He trusts those in the Fortune 500; all others pay on an advance-retainer basis. He does not worry about being paid by large, creditworthy clients but he recognizes that small, somewhat underfunded clients may encounter difficulties paying in a timely fashion or even paying at all. Most of his work is done on an hourly and daily fee basis. Consequently, most clients are served on an advance-retainer basis. The clients deposit funds in advance and he invoices against such deposits, sending invoices as frequently as necessary. His clients understand that he will continue to deliver services as long as funds on deposit are adequate.

On very short assignments, it may be appropriate or necessary to collect all or a very large percentage of the fee before any services are delivered. Many professionals find that a degree of certainty about being paid, and paid on time, is helpful to their motivation. They find that they don't work as well if they have to worry about payment. On the other hand, most find it a poor motivational practice to collect the entire fee from the client prior to commencing work (except on very short assignments).

Desiring front-end retainers and start-up payments is quite different from getting them. Success requires above-average negotiating skills. And successful negotiating requires an attitude of indifference. If the client perceives that the professional is hungry and in need of the prospective business, it will be difficult or impossible to obtain a front-end payment. To be successful, the professional must convince the client that a start-up payment is an essential condition and that the professional will walk if the client finds such a policy unacceptable. The more the client perceives that the professional is essential to the project's success, the more likely it is that such payments will be made. If the client believes that the professional is not unique or especially skilled and that the necessary services are widely available elsewhere, the professional is likely to encounter difficulty in obtaining funds up front.

One professional has enjoyed great success in getting start-up payments by establishing a firm policy that services will not be provided in its absence. She will walk away from potential business where the client refuses to provide an advance retainer. This policy is communicated strongly but tastefully. She looks the client directly in the eye and says, "A deposit of 30 percent of the total fee as an advance retainer is required before I commence work." For her, this is not a request, but a command. Often her clients ask to receive special treatment. She refuses. In more than 75 percent of the cases, the client pays the requested start-up fee; she does not concern herself with the others. Early in her professional career she was more flexible and accommodating. The experience of working for free and expending valuable time trying to collect fees caused her to realize that a firm policy is right for her. Let the nature of your practice and the unique expectations of your clients dictate a policy appropriate for your circumstances.

Q78
Should I ever cut my fee to get the business?

Never cut your fee to get the business, even if you need the income. Some clients will ask you to reduce your fee, a request that may mean many things. In some cases, it may be a sincere need on the part of the client to reduce the expense of obtaining your services. But it may also be a means for the client to say that he does not wish to make use of your services. Without saying so directly, the client is hopeful that a request to reduce the fee will cause you to sever the relationship. In addition, a good number of prospective clients will simply request a fee reduction to test your willingness to accept a lower rate of compensation. They calculate that if you are sufficiently hungry and in need of the business they will save dollars.

So, be prepared to have a ready answer for the client who questions the size of your fee. When the client is trying to get you to shave the fee for your services, always remember the following rules:

1. If you are willing to cut your fee, without a corresponding cut in the scope of the work, the client will feel that your fees were artificially inflated to begin with. Lowering your fee will only raise further questions like: Could I have negotiated a better deal?

2. If you cut your fee, for the same scope of work, you are telling the client that you feel your services are worth less.

3. Cutting the fee on the promise that more, better, and bigger business will follow later runs the almost certain risk that the client will always try to chisel you out of your deserved fee. It worked once, why not try it again? And in most cases, the client will communicate your "flexibility" to others, further compounding your reputation for being "very flexible."

4. Willingness to accept a lower fee says that you have no other options for your time and are hungry for the business. This serves to destroy the competence the client perceived you to have.

A firm way to deal with the request for a lower fee is to cut the fee to the level the client can afford without hurting your image or agreeing to work for less than the value of your time:

> I fully understand that your budget is limited to $8,000, and that making a commitment to expend the $9,306 I have proposed may not be possible at this time. It would, of course, be possible to handle the problem you have described, within your budget; perhaps even for a little less. To bring the project in at $8,000 or less I would suggest the following changes in what I have proposed (describe the various tasks that would be eliminated or reduced). The impact on your project would be as follows (describe the ways in which the reduced project would be less effective or useful than the original).

By proposing a reduction in the scope of the work, you are accommodating the client's budget requirements, at the same time preserving your image and not agreeing to work for less than the value of your time. As another side benefit of this approach the client may realize that the reduced scope of work will yield less than the desired results and somehow find the extra $1,306 in the budget to compensate you for the original project and get what was really desired.

In the above example, note that the original quoted fee was $9,306. Quoting an odd number rather than a rounded figure for a fixed-price project tells the client that you worked with actual costs, not approximate ones, and that you used a sharp pencil in making your calculations. Resist the tendency to round up (or down). If the total cost of performing the work is $10,511, quote that figure, not

$10,500; even though you rounded down, the client is apt to sus-
pect otherwise. If the actual cost is a round figure, perhaps $9,100,
quote an odd number ($9,103 or $9,107). The numerical difference
is slight, but the figure will be much more credible.

Q79
*To what extent will increasing my fee result in my losing clients and
business?*

Increasing fees is necessary and expected, and if your increases are
reasonable, you should not expect to lose either prospective or
existing clients. However, the key word is reasonable. Prices these
days seem to be always on the increase, establishing a certain
"inflation mentality" that is a help to you, but increases should not
occur too frequently. You want to avoid the impression that every
time your client turns around your fees are up again. Thus, limit
your increase in fees to once a year, or at the absolute most—when
prices are accelerating rapidly—twice a year. Your increases should
be sufficiently well-calculated and substantial to last (six to) twelve
months.

When you raise your fees, ask yourself, "Am I just creaming
the market, or are there legitimate reasons why my clients should
pay more for the services provided?" If there are good reasons,
communicate them to your clients. Informing regular clients by letter about 90 days in advance of a fee increase will give ample notice
for client planning and will spur those thinking about making use
of your services to get down to business now rather than wait.
When informing clients that fees will be increased, you may want
to include an explanation in your letter. Point out all of the factors
that have given rise to increased rates: rent, utilities, secretarial
assistance, increased self-employment taxes, etc. If your justifica-
tions are reasonable and well-communicated, you should have little
trouble convincing your clients of the necessity of your increase.
Remember, however, clients don't really care about your problems.
A fee increase, if perceived as reasonable, will be accepted as long
as the client feels the services provided are beneficial. Thus, you
may also wish to point out the benefits produced in the past and
the accomplishments that may be anticipated in the future.

When raising fees, think about providing a benefit to existing clients or prospects that you are currently marketing. Send out a letter that states that fees will be raised on a specific date but that for existing clients or active prospects fees will be raised on a later date. Or indicate that any business committed to prior to a given date will be honored at the existing (lower) fee. You will find that many tentative prospects will become solid clients, and existing clients will decide to retain you for further services now rather than later.

One final note. If you are not fully convinced of the wisdom of your decision to increase fees, you will communicate your uncertainty and (perhaps) embarrassment to the client. This, possibly more than other factors, will hinder your ability to win client acceptance of your fee increase. Once you have made your decision, stick to it. Do not start indiscriminately cutting fees for clients who cannot understand your well-justified, much needed, and very reasonable increase.*

Q80
Should I charge indirect expenses separately or include them in my fee?

Take care in quoting fees and invoicing to be sure you don't communicate that you are in any way petty or not delivering solid benefits. Almost all clients would prefer to pay a little more per hour or day than be burdened by many small service charges for support services, activities, and costs they feel should be included in the already high fee they are paying. A feeling that fees are reasonable and predictable, and that invoices are not full of "nickel and dime" surprises, will encourage referrals and future direct business.

---

*One professional elected to double the fee charged clients. He did so because he found that in conducting proprietary seminars he could make a daily profit that was about equal to the new higher fee. He believed that his decision would result in the loss of several clients and that those remaining would reduce the number of hours per month that his services were engaged. This did not concern him because of the option he had to conduct seminars. Thus, he was able to communicate his new fee structure with great confidence and indifference. He discovered that no clients left him and none cut back his hours. Undoubtedly he had undervalued his services in setting the original fee, but his confidence no doubt contributed to his success in getting clients to pay the higher fee. Many professionals, this one included, regularly underestimate the value of their services to clients.

Routine and nominal expenses such as photocopies, telephone calls, postage, etc., are best included in a slightly higher hourly or daily rate fee. This avoids the feeling on the part of the client that you are petty and expensive. Needless to say, such an approach will greatly reduce your internal bookkeeping.

Major and special outlays, which are really direct expenses, should be added to fees. Thus, the cost of a special mailing of perhaps 100 press-release packages on behalf of the client or overnight delivery charges (at the client's request) should be added to the fee. And because they are necessary, expected, and undertaken specifically for the client, such special charges are not unreasonable.

Q81
How should I charge for travel expenses?

Charge for travel expenses (hotel, meals, ground transportation, tips, phone calls, and reasonable incidentals) on a per diem basis rather than a direct reimbursement basis. Most clients prefer the simplicity of per diems, and per diems avoid any criticism about how you spend expense dollars. Think about having multiple per diem rates—one for large, expensive cities where the cost of living is higher and the other for smaller, inexpensive places. The following are two typical per diem rates, the first for a large, expensive city and the second for a smaller city:

Hotel room	$170
Breakfast	10
Lunch	12
Dinner	25
Local transportation	18
Other expenses	15
PER DIEM	$250

Hotel room	$ 88
Breakfast	9
Lunch	10
Dinner	18
Local transportation	12
Other expenses	13
PER DIEM	$150

It is reasonable that a given professional might use both of these per diem rates depending on where he is on assignment. If your practice necessitates travel to locations such as New York City, Tokyo, or London, you might even have a third per diem rate to ensure that you are fairly reimbursed.

Ground transportation can fluctuate greatly depending upon mode of travel and the distance of airport to hotel, etc. It may be more appropriate to exclude local transportation and receive direct reimbursement for all travel expenditures. Even with per diem rates, such expenditures as air tickets, rental cars, and the like are directly reimbursed unless they are added in because of the repeat nature of the travel locations. For example, if your client has you go to Chicago from Boston every other week for an entire year, it would be fairly easy to come up with a flat travel rate that would include your air fare.

When you are away from your home office or the client's office on assignment but will return to your home base before night, the per diem rate will be different. Here, you must cover costs such as meals, phone calls, etc., but not hotel. Many corporations, government agencies, and large professional practices have developed sophisticated systems of payment based upon the number of hours away from the place of residence. One such system works this way:

0– 3 Hours	No payment of per diem.
3– 6 Hours	$25
6–10 Hours	$40
10–15 Hours	$60
15+ Hours	Full per diem. $150

In establishing a per diem rate, it might not be a bad idea to talk to the client to determine what rate is being set for the client organization's key management and executive personnel.

Q82
Is it possible to charge for travel time?

The issue of whether or not to charge for travel time, and at what rate, is primarily a function of the professional's specialty and degree of expertise. If the professional's skills are sufficiently unique, in short supply and great demand, and/or the professional is a prominent and renowned authority, he may be able to charge for travel time at the normal rate for services without encountering any resistance. However, a professional whose skills are more commonplace and readily available from others will have little chance of charging for travel time, and if he does charge—even at a reduced rate—will likely encounter opposition from the client.

Some professionals who are hesitant to charge directly for travel time function on a dual-rate structure, with one billing rate for local clients and a higher rate for out-of-town clients. This dual approach provides compensation for travel time without the client's awareness, thus lessening or eliminating resistance to the charge.

Q83

Does conducting a feasibility study for a client generally result in additional business?

One of the most effective marketing tools a professional can use is the feasibility study. Feasibility studies help the professional get a foot in the door, and they give clients the chance to assess the need to take action and determine relatively quickly how effective the professional will be in handling the problem.

Many clients are reluctant to commit to a long-term or sizeable project. If you sense that your client is reluctant to engage your services for the "total project proposed," you can always propose to conduct a feasibility study first and consider additional services later. In this way, the feasibility study provides the client with an opportunity to assess your skills before making a larger financial commitment.

To be effective, a feasibility study must be done properly. It is not a needs analysis, which only points out the need to take some action, feasible or not. Neither is it the same as an evaluation, which assesses effectiveness or efficiency. Rather, a feasibility study helps the client determine a reasonable result that can be achieved given certain resources and boundaries of investigation.

A professional is in the position to offer a client essentially two options:

1. Tell me what it is you want to accomplish, and I'll tell you what it will cost.

2. Tell me how much you have to spend, and I'll tell you what you'll get.

Clients can often describe what they want, but they may want far more than they can afford. This is true for the scope of a feasibility study too. Nothing prohibits a series of feasibility studies. After the completion of each, the client can determine the advisability of proceeding further.

Assist the client to determine what information is really needed in establishing the reliability (accuracy) of the information. Don't insist on providing clients with more than they need. Doing so may cause you to lose the business and it violates one of the essentials of ethical, successful practice—placing the client's needs and interests above any others, even your own.

Keep these guidelines in mind to help ensure quality feasibility studies:

1. Know the cost and value of information. Find out enough to make a meaningful recommendation, but don't overresearch.

2. Make sure you have adequate resources to conduct the study.

3. Don't propose solutions that cannot be implemented. Study how your client has performed in the past. Don't expect individuals to do things foreign to their nature.

4. Make certain the risk involved in the course of action recommended is not out of proportion to the likely gain.

5. Communicate the impact of not taking action. Be sure the client knows the potential harm of delaying a decision or action.

Q84
Should I provide my prospect with a proposal even when not specifically asked for one?

Don't look upon having to write a proposal as a waste of time or unnecessary drudgery. Research clearly shows that those who write proposals (even when they don't have to) wind up getting bigger and better assignments.

Develop proposal writing skills that are right for marketing your services. The kind of proposal you must write to get the business is different from most proposals. Your proposal is unique. It is designed to get business. If you learned your proposal writing skills within an organization where proposals were primarily designed to inform, you are probably writing the wrong kind of proposal. It will cost you in lost business.

Although not always required, the written proposal is often an important part of selling your services. However, you need to learn to write persuasive proposals without giving away free advice. The following are a few suggestions for when the proposal should be used and what it should communicate:

1. The proposal should be developed only when you believe that a sufficiently good opportunity for business exists, one that justifies the expenditure of time and effort. Budget time and dollars to be invested in proposal writing activity; this will encourage you to spend the time necessary in writing proposals.

2. The proposal must communicate your ideas so that the reader (decision-maker) is convinced that you can achieve what you propose within the budget estimate or fixed price you quote. Thus, you must be persuasive, convincing, honest, and believable.

3. The proposal must convince your client of the following:
   a. The need for your services is important, even essential, and failure to address the need or problem will have an adverse impact on the client's interest.
   b. Your objectives and the general approach suggested will correct the problem, take advantage of the opportunity, and reduce or eliminate the need.
   c. The procedures you advocate will accomplish the objectives and are the best and/or only appropriate alternative for solving the problem or reducing the need. It should be quite clear to the prospect that no other procedure would be as effective and efficient, or have a greater probability of success.

4. The proposal must emphasize the desirable and beneficial
    results of the services you will provide and avoid dwelling on
    the detailed technology and strategy that will accomplish the
    results. You want your proposal to sell your services, not pro-
    vide a recipe for the client to solve the problem without you.

Professional-service proposals are usually divided into three
sections (at least conceptually): the front section, the main section,
and the conclusion.

The front section is designed to lead the reader into the main
section and should convey your understanding of the purposes of
the services being provided, the client's need for your services, the
objectives and purposes that will guide your work, and the specific
accomplishments that will result. In addition, it is here that you
create in the client's mind a mandate for action and assure the client that you alone are the best choice to meet the client's needs.
You should also include a statement of assurances, telling your client that there are no lawsuits or judgments pending against you;
all your costs are true and reasonable; you do not discriminate in
hiring; you self-insure and hold your client blameless and will
defend any lawsuits, etc.

The main section explains, without being too detailed or
instructive, how you will meet the objectives. In many cases, it contains three elements: a pictorial description (often in the form of a
functional flow diagram) of the work you will do; a time line that
communicates to the client a schedule of the work; and a narrative
statement that describes the diagram and details the results, accomplishments, and benefits to be achieved by your work. It may also
summarize the general approach to be applied, first revealed in the
front section.

The main section is the heart of the proposal, at least as a selling tool. It is here that you demonstrate your conceptual approach
and clearly and persuasively explain the benefits to be achieved.

The conclusion may contain plans and procedures for evaluation of and/or reporting on the services you advocate, a statement
of your experience and capabilities, as well as an explanation of the
mechanics of engaging your services—fees, invoicing, payment
procedures, etc. The conclusion should also provide a persuasive
summation of why the client should retain your services.

Your proposal may be your final selling opportunity, and as such, it should reflect the professional quality of your work. Without appearing lavish, good-quality cover stock, paper, and binding will enhance the client's favorable impression of your proposal and your chances of gaining their business. As a rule of thumb, your proposal should be of a quality and look that is about equivalent to the quality your client would provide to one of their customers or clients.*

Q85
How can I make my proposal stand out from those of my competitors?

Here are some suggestions to make your proposal remembered and talked about when being compared to those submitted by the competition.

1. Put a summary or abstract in front of your narrative section. Many proposals are complex and lengthy and fail to communicate the main point, confusing the prospective client. A summary or abstract will help to ensure that the prospect clearly understands the proposal.

2. Avoid jargon whenever possible. One professional's proposal, full of jargon, made mention of a "fully articulated horizontal and vertical education curriculum." Would you know one if you saw one? If you must use a technical term, define it. If you must use an acronym, first give the full name, then the acronym in parentheses; for example, National Organization for Women (NOW); thereafter you can refer to it as NOW.

3. Use simple declarative sentences. When you find a sentence that goes on and on, go back and rework it. Clear writing will increase your proposal's readability and saleability.

4. Get the reader's attention. Use something catchy, different, provocative. Consider raising a thought-provoking question; it encourages the reader to seek the answer.

---

*Detailed step-by-step procedures (and examples) for writing client-producing proposals will be found in *The Contract and Fee-Setting Guide for Consultants & Professionals* (John Wiley and Sons, 1990), by Howard L. Shenson, CMC.

5. Summarize complex ideas quickly; provide detail later.

6. Provide meaningful evidence as to why your idea should be considered.   Appeal to a number of motivations, such as how your idea or concept will improve profit, increase productivity, ward off regulators, etc.

7. Close by not only asking the prospect to take action but by spelling out the precise action that should be taken. Provide options, if appropriate.

8. If you are unsure the client is able to afford all that you have proposed, consider dividing your proposal into two or more segments, allowing the prospect to select from the range of services you are offering.

If you have developed a proposal for new business that falls through, identify who else whould benefit from such services and recycle your proposal to others.

Q86
Is it advantageous to combine a proposal and contract?

While some professionals believe that it saves time and clarifies communications to combine the contractual terms and conditions of the project with a proposal, most find it advantageous to separate the proposal and the contract. Why? Contracts usually contain provisions that create (potential) obligations and requirements for the client that may interfere with marketing.

A good contract, one that protects you and your client's interests, contains clauses that, if introduced early in the decision-making process, make doing business with you seem less desirable than the prospective client may have thought. Since it is not to your benefit to introduce anything that may negate marketing effectiveness, contractual matters are best introduced after the client has made a decision to engage your professional services.

First sell the client on the technical merits and beneficial results of the services you will be providing. Then, once the client is convinced that you are the right choice for the right fee, introduce and gain acceptance of terms and provisions such as the dates when payments will be made (including advance or up front retainers), when deliveries will be made, what happens if the client does not pay, etc. Once the client has decided to retain your services, such provisions are more likely to be seen as small nuisances rather than reasons not to do business.

Q87
Is a written agreement with my client always necessary?

It is always in your interest to work with a written contract or agreement. Aside from the obvious legal protection such a contract provides you and your client, there are many other advantages. One of the important advantages of a written contract is that it demonstrates to the client that you take your own business responsibilities seriously. The natural expectation is that you will take care of the client's business with equal seriousness. No one says that the contract has to be formal or fancy; with some clients and with certain types of services a simple letter of agreement should do the trick (though any contract, formal or informal, should be checked by an attorney). Putting in writing the essence and particulars of your agreement has another important advantage in that it clarifies communications, expectations, and responsibilities; causes both professional and client to remember more clearly and behave more predictably; and is invaluable should a misunderstanding or dispute occur.

The contract or letter of agreement should only be prepared once the client has agreed to the proposed work. And it is rarely in your interest to combine a proposal and contract.

Include in every contract and agreement a paragraph communicating the client's responsibilities and obligations—everything that you depend upon from timely payment of invoices to the provision of documents, working space, and secretarial support. In long-term contracts, protect your interests by including a cost-of-living clause that will maintain your income should inflation become significant. In all contracts, spell out the terms and conditions for payment. When money becomes tight, 30 days often becomes 60 or 90 days. While making terms of payment a matter of contractual agreement does not ensure compliance, it is regarded as more meaningful than trade custom and can help you to collect fees in a more timely fashion.

While it is certainly in your interest to protect yourself in the contract, it is to your benefit and your client's benefit that the contract be as protective or more protective of the client's interest as it is of yours. Such evident concern for the client will enhance client confidence in the wisdom of having retained your services, increase the chances of doing further business in the future, and engender further referrals.

Thus, the written contract should spell out both the client's and the professional's responsibilities before, during, and after the provision of services. You will also want to include stipulations and conditions for termination of the agreement, subcontracting, insurance coverage, liability, assignment, arbitration, and other concerns appropriate to the circumstances.

Whether you choose to have a formal document drafted or simply to write a letter of agreement, make the terms and conditions as straightforward, unambiguous, and specific as possible to avoid any misunderstandings and to achieve a productive and harmonious relationship.

Q88
Should I require clients to sign a contract for a short consultation?

While a written contract or agreement is almost always advisable in any professional engagement, sometimes your services are retained for such a short period of time that a formal agreement (signed by both parties) would really seem out of place or not worth the investment of time to draft and negotiate. However, you should provide the client with a letter of confirmation or engagement that specifies the terms and conditions of your work together. This is not really a contract, as the client has not indicated acceptance, but it does set the parameters of the relationship. Such a letter might also be used prior to development of a formal agreement for a more comprehensive assignment.

There are several features that a letter of engagement should contain. Chief among them are the following:

1. Acknowledgment of the time and place the first formal/work meeting will take place.

2. Specification of the purpose of the first meeting and the purpose of the consultation in general.

3. An estimated time line for the project, or a statement as to why it is not possible to provide such an estimate.

4. A communication as to what the fee will be for the services to be provided, if possible, or an indication of the basis on which the fee will be charged.

5. Specification of the payment arrangements as well as the invoice schedule. In the past, many professionals have tended to be satisfied by just telling clients when the invoice will be sent, leaving so-called "trade custom" to govern when payments will be made. During periods of tight credit, "net, 30 days" can turn into 60 to 90 days or more. It is a good idea to inform the client of the date when payment is required.

Figure 7-1 is an example of a letter of confirmation or engagement that might be sent to a client meeting at your office for a short consultation.

Q89
Should I have a hold harmless clause in my contract?

The decision to include a clause limiting your liability in the agreement with your client should be considered with great care. Limiting your liability though contractual agreements is not a cure-all but perhaps one of a variety of tools employed to protect the professional. Combined with caution in selecting clients, professional liability insurance and other vehicles for protecting yourself, it can be a help. However, remember that a contract is only between the

SAMPLE LETTER OF ENGAGEMENT

Name of Client
Company
Address
City/State/Zip

Dear _____:

I am writing to confirm our appointment at 10:00 a.m. on Tuesday, November 3rd.

The purpose of this meeting will be to discuss the specifics relating to the feasibility study which I will undertake on behalf of the _____ proposal.

Following this meeting, I will commence the feasibility study. It is my expectation that the total time to complete the study will be about seventy (70) hours.

Please be advised that the fee for my services will be one hundred and fifty dollars ($150) per hour plus expenses incurred on your behalf in connection with the study.

The payment of fees may be handled in either of two ways:

    o You may deposit an advance retainer with me and I shall invoice against the retainer, or

    o I will invoice for services performed and expenses incurred on a weekly basis. Invoices will be prepared and mailed on each Friday. The payment of the invoice will be made by you not later than the following Friday.

If the terms of this letter meet with your understanding and agreement, I would appreciate your signing below and returning a copy of this letter in the envelope provided not later than October 27th.

I look forward to working with you on this assignment.

Sincerely,

_____

Name of Professional

Approved _____

Date _____

Figure 7-1   Sample letter of engagement.

parties to the document; you can't remove third-party rights. The nature of the services provided and the laws of the jurisdiction in which you do business determine whether such a clause has any value. This is an issue worth discussing with legal counsel.

Most importantly, contractual limitations on liability can hinder your marketing effectiveness. Such limitations are definitely not a strong selling point relative to the client's perception of the quality and care of your services. Perhaps the chief drawback to the hold harmless clause is that it raises the issue of professional error or omission; it raises these matters in such a fashion that the client has to consider seriously the potential consequences. Often, it is not to the professional's benefit to include a hold harmless clause and run the risk of raising such concerns with a prospect.

As far as the content of a hold harmless agreement is concerned, it is usually determined by the nature of the situation and the kinds of harm that might surface. The following example may be useful for general guidance in developing one suitable for your purposes.

> NAME OF CLIENT ORGANIZATION will defend NAME OF PROFESSIONAL, its officers, directors, partners, owners, agents, affiliates, or employees against and hold them and each of them harmless from all loss, liability, or expense (including, but not limited to, reasonable attorneys' fees and costs), without exception, arising from (1) claims or causes of action alleging negligence or breach of warranty; (2) infringement or alleged infringement of patents, copyrights, trademarks, or trade names; (3) any violation of privacy or publicity; (4) any violation of any federal or state "consumer protection legislation"; (5) any unfair trade practices; (6) any civil, criminal, administrative, or other action or proceeding brought or taken by the United States or any state or any agency thereof related to any services, merchandise or advertising claims or representations related to any agreement, arrangement, or understanding between NAME OF CLIENT ORGANIZATION and NAME OF PROFESSIONAL.

Any such proposed hold harmless agreement should be reviewed by legal counsel. The laws of some jurisdictions can serve to make a contract voidable if certain rights are given up by the contracting parties. Sometimes courts fail to recognize contractual limits, particularly when the client is unsophisticated and the professional experienced. They may hold the view that the professional took undue advantage of the client.

Also, just because you have developed a hold harmless agreement and had it reviewed by your attorney does not mean it must be used in every situation. It is an optional clause that you may elect to use in certain circumstances.

Q90
How frequently should I invoice my clients?

To a certain extent the frequency of invoicing is governed by professional custom or prevailing practice within your geographic area. You should be familiar with both.

Invoice frequently. Many smaller bills are more likely to be paid than one or two large bills. Bill on time. Don't store up charges and don't be late in sending out invoices.

Your invoice should be fully explanatory. Let the invoice answer all of the questions that will be asked when it is received. Figures 7-2 and 7-3 present two sample invoices showing you the difference between one that itemizes and justifies the expenses to the client (and, therefore, will be more acceptable to the client) and one that merely asks for payment.

Since both of these invoices ask for the same amount to be paid, what difference do these "style alternatives" make?

1. The first invoice is addressed to the client personally. If he is away for a few days on business, it may be placed on a desk unopened until the client returns, which may delay payment.

2. Even though both invoices ask for the same dollar amount, the first invoice looks much more unreasonable than the second. The second documents the time expended by the professional, and while $1,100+ for the week sounds expensive, when the client sees what it is for, it seems more reasonable.

3. The first invoice does not say when payment is due. Your contract with the client should specify when invoices will be sent and when payments are due, but it does not hurt to remind the

```
TO:    Name
       Title
       Firm
       Address
       City/State/Zip

Invoice Number:    555A                Invoice Date: May 15, 19XX


Professional Services Rendered
    May 8 - 14, 19XX............................................... $1135.00


Direct Expenses:
    Automobile Mileage.................................................   26.40
    Long Line Charges..................................................    4.45
    Dinner with Attorney...............................................   26.70


Total Due........................................................... $1192.55
```

Figure 7-2   Sample of a non-itemized invoice.

controller or bookkeeper about the date; this person may not remember what it says in the contract and, in fact, may never have seen it. Note that the second invoice says in two ways— "Net 10 Days" and "Due and Payable by May 25, 19XX"— when payment should be made. Most people, even your client's bookkeeper, will do what they are told to do, so remember to tell them.

4. The second invoice is signed, suggesting to the client that the invoice was sent as a conscious effort. It indicates that someone in your firm in a position of authority and responsibility— you—looked at and approved it.

When working on a fixed-price or fixed-fee contract, it is usually not necessary to detail the specific charges. The invoice format presented in Figure 7-4 is illustrative.

Be sure to let the client know early in the assignment—and before the assignment has started, if possible—just what the fee is likely to be. Don't be afraid to talk dollars whenever necessary. Some professionals avoid talking money because they find such discussions difficult or embarrassing. However, it is an essential part of your total involvement and it sets client expectations.

```
TO:    Firm                              INVOICE NUMBER:  555A
       Attn:    Name                     INVOICE DATE:    May 15, 19XX
                Title                     TERMS:           Net, 10 days
       Address
       City/State/Zip
```

Professional Services:

```
05-08-XX    Preparation of Final Planning Documents and Planning
            Report Status Forms...3 hours.........................  $300.00

05-09-XX    Telephone consultation with Mr. Greer...
            21 minutes............................................    35.00

05-10-XX    Presentation of Planning Documents to
            Executive Committee...4 hours.........................   400.00

05-10-XX    Meeting with Corporate Attorney...3 hours..............  300.00

05-11-XX    Telephone consultation
            with Ms Sanders...1 hour..............................   100.00


TOTAL PROFESSIONAL SERVICES.......................................  $1135.00
```

Direct Expenses:

```
Automobile Mileage...132 miles @ $0.20 ...........................    26.40
Long Line Charges, telephone call of 05-09-89.....................     4.45
Dinner with Corporate Attorney on 05-10-89........................    26.70
     (Receipt attached)


TOTAL DUE AND PAYABLE BY MAY 25, 19XX.............................  $1192.55



              Authorized Signature _____
```

Figure 7-3   Sample of an itemized invoice.

Q91
Will progress reports assist me in being paid in a timely fashion?

Professionals often experience difficulty in being paid on time and without question. A number of strategies, including the submission

```
Firm                                 Invoice No:   _____
Attn:    Name
         Title                           Date:     _____
Address
City/State/Zip                          Terms:  Net, 10 days

-----------------------------------------------------------------------

Scheduled Contract Payment

     Number 3, Contract No. 6501..............................  $ 2,850.00



     TOTAL DUE AND PAYABLE ON OR BEFORE May XX, 19XX............  $ 2,850.00



     Authorized Signature  _____
```

Figure 7-4 Sample invoice on a fixed-fee contract.

of interim progress reports, will help. There is an art to impressing the client that the fees charged are reasonable and just in relation to the professional services that have been provided. A client who feels that your fee is fair and more than equal to the results achieved is far more likely to retain your services again or refer you to others.

You will encourage satisfaction by working with a written contract or agreement, setting and disclosing fees in a way that reflects the value of the benefits you are providing, and making sure that your work is superlative. Communication is the key. Frequently, professionals learn that the individual responsible for paying the invoice is someone other than the person with whom the professional interfaces personally or technically. The person approving the bill often lacks appreciation for the many hours or days of efforts that have been expended to produce the results. The professional or consultant must take pains to explain on a regular and consistent basis to key personnel within the client organization just what it is that he is doing and the effort involved.

One technique that works well is the weekly or monthly status memo or interim report. This report need not be lengthy, but it should follow a format—something such as:

Date.
Period of time this report covers.
Status at the beginning of this report period.
Accomplishments during this period.
Status at the end of the reporting period.
Problems and difficulties encountered during this period.
Problems and difficulties anticipated in the future.
Summary of activities to be provided in the next period.

If the person who will approve your invoice is not the key technical or management contact for you in the client organization, you should send a copy of the report or memo (with prior permission) to the individual who will approve your invoice as well as to your principal contact. Don't set up a situation in which the person who will approve your invoice hears from and about you on only two occasions—when the contract is signed and when the invoice is sent. Keep communicating.

Another benefit of this memo or report is that your contact within the client's organization is regularly informed as to your activities and progress and may be able to provide assistance in

---

In business it sometimes becomes necessary to play a "bad guy" role. This may be in connection with fee collection, insistence on providing services in a particular fashion, turning down business, ending a relationship with a client, etc. Whenever possible try to separate the bad guy role from the good guy role by having these unpleasant tasks handled by a third party. If you have a partner, associate, or assistant, it is probably in your interest to let him or her play the bad guy for you and vice versa. This tactic allows you to extricate yourself while limiting the negative impact on future business or referral opportunities.

areas of difficulty you may encounter in the future. Communicating such a report is a nice professional touch on your part. It will also help you to be better organized, anticipate problems, and do better planning.

One further benefit is worth mentioning. If your contact is likely to encounter questions from superiors or peers—"What is that consultant (attorney, architect, financial planner, etc.) doing anyway?"—he has a ready source of information to answer the questions. Don't underestimate the importance of informing your client of assignment status to enable him to inform others.

Q92
How can I avoid the requirement of having to write a final report?

You probably shouldn't try. A final report—when you are working on a discrete project—can be advantageous to future business. Even if not requested, you should probably write one anyway. Reporting the findings or results of the project is the culmination of the effort that first began with marketing. It may require a substantial investment of both time and effort but is a valuable work product to the client, and you should be compensated for your efforts.

The goal of the project is the guidance of those with problems or needs who have retained your services. Only if the report gives the client guidance and understanding and establishes the conviction that its conclusions are correct can we say that the services have been provided successfully.

And what determines success? Not the professional's receipt of the agreed-upon fee (however important to you). The success of any project depends upon your ability to accomplish the objectives agreed to with the client, at approximately the cost, and within the time frame agreed upon at the outset of the project. Successful assignments, therefore, are the direct result of your performance. However, success is also dependent upon your ability to communicate effectively what has occurred. If the client does not fully understand what you have done, the project has not been successfully accomplished.

Despite the paramount importance of written final reports, it is not at all uncommon for professionals to shy away from writing them. They are time-consuming, and documentation of what has been done is far from the most interesting professional activity. But the final report has great value to both client and professional and, thus, you should make every effort to provide a final report. Large corporate clients and government agencies almost always require a final report; smaller clients often need you to explain the benefits to justify the added expense.

The following are potential benefits to the client:

1. The report will provide written evidence that the project has been carried out, that is, that the service has been delivered, and an indication as to the success achieved in meeting the client's objectives.

2. The report will document in a formal fashion your conclusions and recommendations. This can be helpful in assisting the client with regard to decision-making, long-range planning, and taking advantage of future opportunities to implement your recommendations.

3. In bringing the data, analysis, and findings into an organized and permanent form, your report is often the only systematic source of documentation for the project. The report may therefore serve as a guide for further study, analysis, and research.

4. The dissemination of the report may serve to provide a "spread effect" throughout the organization for your ideas. In case of a change of management or administration, the ideas and results of your project can continue to be implemented and to benefit your client.

5. The dissemination of your report demonstrates to upper management and to the client's colleagues the wisdom of having retained your services.

The following are potential benefits to the professional:

1. The report serves as a reminder of your contributions and will increase the probability of repeat and/or referral business.

2. The report may allow your ideas to be implemented by other departments and/or organizations, who may choose to retain your services at a future date.

3. The quality of the services provided is often judged by the quality of the report. This is particularly true when third persons, not directly involved in the project, will be placed in the position of making recommendations on your findings or evaluating your efforts.

4. The effectiveness with which the report communicates may well determine whether the client chooses to implement your ideas.

If the potential rewards of preparing a written report indicate that it is an effective use of your time, and if the report is not mandated by the client organization, you may wish to market the final report as a part of the total package of services you provide. Market the benefits that the client will receive from the final report and emphasize those benefits that you believe your potential client is most interested in. You must be specific and convincing, as the client is to be charged, either directly or indirectly, for all of the time that you spend in preparing and presenting the final report. If the client cannot pay for the preparation and presentation of a final report, it is appropriate to suggest that a verbal report be given in its place. This is also an excellent means to decrease the cost of the total contract without being asked to reduce your fees, in the event

---

Develop the ability to create unspoken, unmentioned referrals. If your responsibilities include drafting final or interim reports, encourage the client to provide as widespread a dissemination of the report as is reasonable. Put together a recommended circulation list and include a rationale for each recommended dissemination category. The very act of disseminating the results of the project casts a favorable image on you and serves as a silent referral.

that the client is unable to afford the full scope of the services you recommend.

Q93
Is there any information that should be excluded from a written (final) report?

Even though you may be asked to prepare a formal written report for a project (or gain client acceptance of your proposal to do so), take care to exclude information that the client would not wish to have documented. You may have to guide the client in determining information that should not be included. Such information might include politically sensitive recommendations or highly confidential data that might be better communicated orally. Also, you may find it necessary to exclude information that discloses in too great detail the methods and strategies you have employed to accomplish the objectives described in your report.

The written final report should likely not be provided if:

1. The expense incurred by the client for doing so is greater than the benefit achieved.
2. There is no need to document accomplishments, or the information is to be distributed to such a small population that other dissemination means are more effective, and/or the client is so involved in the project that he already has intimate, detailed knowledge of the entire project.
3. The information is of a such a nature—sensitive, proprietary, etc.—that it would best not be conveyed in writing.

Writing a final report when one is not needed is a waste of your valuable time and the client's resources, and might suggest to the client that the report is being provided for the sole objective of generating additional billings. This may cause the client to question the benefit of the entire project and reduce your future business opportunities or referrals.

Q94
How can I find time to do really creative work with all of the daily interruptions?

Time management is more of a problem for professionals than for most in our society. Because of the added dimensions of uncertainty about the ebb and flow of future business and the likely prospect of unforeseen demands by existing and new clients, a surprising number of professionals and consultants find time-management problems sufficiently stressful to endanger the economic health of their practices.

Time management is a rather personal thing. What works for you may not work for someone else. This simple observation is probably the reason that the market provides so many time-management systems, devices, and training programs. Here are some time-management techniques demonstrated to be effective for professionals. Pick and choose. Better, try all that seem reasonable and discard those that do not fit your style:

1. Recognize that creativity comes in spurts. Abandon, for the time, those projects that require intense creativity until you are in a creative mode. Sitting around looking at a blank piece of paper creates a time loss that you will never recover.

2. Plan each day. Taking ten minutes first thing in the morning or last thing at night to plan will make the day far more productive. Don't fall prey to the belief that self-discipline won't work for you.

3. Block out times for undisturbed work. Do not take phone calls or other interruptions for 90 minutes to two hours. The world will wait until you're ready for them and your productivity will increase. Alternative: Some professionals report excellent results from blocking out entire days; they are simply inaccessible on Tuesdays and Fridays, for example.

4. Avoid appointment fatigue. Schedule appointments for one or two days a week and refuse to meet with people on other days unless it is absolutely vital. Do not tell people who want to meet with you that this is a time-management system you have adopted. Tell them you are already committed for those days. It makes you seem more desirable (busy) and accomplishes your purpose.

5. Live with being a deadline junky.   Some people do their best and most creative work under extreme deadline pressure. If that's you, recognize and live with it. It is one of your strong advantages, and you should not feel guilty or try to change your behavior to satisfy the dictates of another's time-management philosophy.

6. Identify your prime time.   People do their best (most creative) work at different times of the day. Some people are early morning people; others, night owls. Turn it to your advantage. If you do your best work between midnight and 4:00 A.M., figure out how to get the rest of the world to adapt to your schedule. Maybe you have several different prime times. Some professionals are erratic. Certain days they are effective in the morning; other days at night. Work when you work best for maximum productivity and creativity.

7. Handle every letter, paper, and call just once.   Refuse to put it down until the problem is solved. Much of the time, stress is the result of mounting, unsolved problems that you are still "considering."

8. It's okay to procrastinate.   Don't feel guilty. Remember that many work best under deadline pressure.

9. Learn to say no.   Whose life is it anyway? Clients and staff members often must be told to give you space. You should arrange your work schedule, your life, your obligations in a fashion that is most productive, rewarding, and enjoyable for you. You cannot be truly productive, creative, or even happy with your lot unless you can say no.

Some simple additional ways to get more productive time out of each week:

o Spend 10 to 12 hours in your office, Monday through Friday.

o Start the work day by arriving at the office no later than 6:00 A.M.

o Force yourself to delegate some portion of every task, no matter how small; approach your work with the attitude of how can I get someone to do this for me.

o Learn speed reading.

o Limit all meetings to less than 45 minutes.

o Work and schedule meetings during meals.

o Spend two or three hours working on Saturday and Sunday, but work early (6:00–9:00 A.M.) to avoid family complaints.

If you want to help your clients to be more productive, instruct them to hold all meetings in rooms without chairs. If you have a staff, try it yourself. Meetings, it has been found, are about 43 percent shorter and just as meaningful, if not more so, if people have to stand while thinking and discussing.

Q95
How can I find time to respond promptly to calls and letters?

Prompt response to all communications and correspondence is an integral part of marketing, serving clients, and managing your practice. You cannot separate writing and replying to letters, making and returning phone calls, from the rest of your business; delays in response will hurt the success of your practice significantly. Respond to all written correspondence received (from clients, prospects, and others) as promptly as possible, and certainly within seven days. If you need more time to give a full answer, at least acknowledge the receipt of the letter and communicate by what date you will be able to provide a substantive response.

And make sure that all correspondence and other written

material leaving your office is clear, concise, grammatically correct, and without spelling or typographical errors. Check, double-check, and have other people check your writing for errors. In this world of careless and incorrect writing (and speech), your carefully drafted, well-written letter will stand out.

In addition, respond to all telephone calls quickly. If possible, return the call on the day received and certainly by the next day. Be prompt and courteous on the phone as well as in writing. The small effort expended will gain you clients and respect.

Today, seemingly countless numbers of executives and professionals fail to return calls or acknowledge correspondence. This is not only unprofessional, but it will have negative economic consequences. However, making time to respond promptly to letters and phone calls is often hard, given the press of client work and marketing responsibilities.

Discipline yourself to spend a set amount of time each day responding to communications. Don't permit yourself to go to lunch or go home for the day if you have not returned phone messages or answered the day's mail. Remember that those who are waiting to hear from you may well be contacting your competitors too. The first to respond will have a greater probability of receiving the business. And, since so many fail to respond promptly, others will find the speed of your responsiveness impressive.

Take steps to automate your practice to speed communications. Develop standard, mostly standard, and partially customized letters that can be used with your word processor or data base management computer software. Consider the advisability of making use of technology such as voice mail, computer bulletin boards, etc.

Q96
Is it preferable to use an answering service, an answering machine, or a voice mail system?

If you lack a full staff of secretaries to answer your phone when you are away, or if you prefer not to answer your own phone, you will need an answering service, a telephone answering machine, or a voice mail system. While many professionals and clients feel that a professional's phone being answered by a machine leaves the caller with a negative impression, few seem to think that an answering service leaves callers with negative feelings.

However, many professionals dislike what they perceive to be the inefficiency or errors that may result from the use of an answering service. To avoid errors and to ensure that your telephone answering service gives the appearance of being your private secretary, follow these guidelines:

1. Select a telephone answering service (TAS) by checking the quality of such services used by others. Look for those services who do a good job. When you find one you like, ask the user for the name.

2. Visit the TAS you have selected and arrange for service. Most services have a large number of switchboards with many different operators; select the board/operator that caused you to select this service and insist that you be put on the same board/assigned to the same operator.

3. Remember that the person who answers your phone is a human being too. About the only contact most of these operators have with the customers of the service is listening to the latter complain about how messages were wrong or the telephone was not answered in a timely fashion. Manage to stop in at the TAS at least once or twice a month. While there, spend a few moments getting to know your operator. The individual who answers your phone is a person, not a machine. Make your operator your friend and show genuine interest and concern. Don't forget Secretaries' Week, holidays, birthdays, etc.

   In doing so, you will stand out from the scores of other people who depend upon this person to answer their phones. Who do you think will get the tender loving care? Won't your line be answered first when several ring simultaneously? Won't the operator try hard to get your messages accurately and go to the trouble of trying to track you down when that vital, all-important phone call comes through?

A few extra minutes out of your busy schedule and a few dollars will make a big difference.

If you do use a telephone answering machine, make it less offensive to the people who find it offensive. Avoid the tendency to be cute. Some owners of these machines don't make it clear to the caller that they are dealing with a mechanical device until the caller is 20 to 30 seconds into the message. For example, don't record a message that begins with, "Hello," followed by a pause. The caller will begin talking and soon feel like a fool after responding to the salutation only to be interrupted by the message that continues "I am not able to come to the telephone . . . "

Explore voice mail options. Since many fully staffed commercial enterprises make extensive use of voice mail, it may be a viable alternative.

Remember that all aspects of your image affect the marketing and selling of your services, and the way clients are treated on the phone, in person, and in correspondence affects your image.

Q97

How do solo practices compare financially to larger professional service firms?

Solo practitioners frequently worry that the differences in billing rates, operating ratios, and marketing strategies in comparison with larger firms may place them at a competitive disadvantage. A survey of 6,998 American and Canadian professionals determined that the size of the practice has little or no significant impact on billing rates or pretax income.* But differences in marketing strategies used and overhead expenses reveal significant disparities between solo practitioners and larger firms.

---

*Reprinted from *The Professional Consultant & Information Marketing Report* newsletter (October, 1989), copyright, Howard L. Shenson, CMC, 20750 Ventura Boulevard, Woodland Hills, CA 91364.

Larger firms find it necessary to expend a greater percentage of their revenue on management and marketing and are more likely to engage in expensive, direct-marketing strategies than the solo professional. That is not to say that large practices avoid the proven-to-be-more-effective indirect marketing approaches; they invest heavily in these too. In follow-up interviews, the majority expressed the belief that indirect strategies support direct strategies, making the latter more productive than they might otherwise be.

There are significant differences with respect to marketing strategies employed. Listed below are the percentage of practices that make "regular" use of several popular marketing strategies. (Note, however, that for the larger practices, the number of individuals involved in any direct marketing activities is usually less than the total number of professionals involved in the practice.)

Percentage of Firms Using Popular Marketing Strategies

	Number of Professionals in Firm			
Strategy	*1*	*2–3*	*4–7*	*8+*
Cold personal calls	44.2	47.8	58.3	70.2
Direct mail brochures/sales letters to cold lists	57.5	60.8	71.4	89.2
No-charge diagnostic services to prequalified leads	41.2	43.5	26.3	19.6
Promotion to similar clients on basis of referrals	49.1	48.8	55.7	66.8
Lectures to civic, trade, and professional groups	15.8	18.9	24.7	44.4
Writing articles, books, newsletters for trade, civic, professional audiences	13.9	20.2	25.5	55.7

Solos must necessarily limit the variety of marketing strategies employed to those they find optimally productive. Larger firms are able to assign key personnel to direct different types of marketing campaigns.

Here is how the respondents differed in overhead expenditures, based on practice size:

Overhead Expenditures

Expense	Percentage of Total Overhead Based on Number of Professionals			
	1	*2–3*	*4–7*	*8 +*
Clerical support	12.9	11.3	10.8	7.8
Office rent	3.7	4.4	4.3	4.5
Telephone and postage	5.3	5.4	5.1	5.2
Automotive	4.6	3.8	3.4	3.1
Employment taxes	12.6	13.1	12.9	12.5
Personnel benefits	12.4	11.2	9.7	11.8
Insurance	0.2	0.3	0.2	0.4
Licenses and taxes	0.2	0.1	0.2	0.2
Professional development	4.4	4.2	3.7	3.1
Dues and subscriptions	0.7	0.5	1.0	0.9
Printing and copying	1.3	1.0	0.9	0.7
Stationery/supplies	0.8	0.6	0.5	0.4
Accounting and legal	1.8	1.5	1.4	0.8
Practice management	8.5	9.4	11.7	13.1
Marketing	26.5	30.2	33.4	34.8
Other	4.1	3.0	0.8	0.7
Total	100.0	100.0	100.0	100.0

Conclusion

Having read this book, you are now familiar with research-based, proven-effective strategies for building a successful professional consulting practice. Continue to study the ideas expressed herein. Some of the strategies and approaches that may not seem appropriate now will seem far more suitable later.

During a presentation to a national professional association, one of the attendees asked an important question: "When all is said and done, what really is the mark of distinction of a highly successful private practice professional?" My reply can be summarized in one word—*indifference.* The truly successful professional consultant is indifferent in a very important sense. He is not pressured to make his services available to a particular client. He is relaxed. The business of any one particular client is not so vital to his financial or professional viability that he must compromise his standards.

Think about it. Would you want to be served by a professional who is so in need of the business that he would advocate services that are not in your best interest? Would a true professional engage in any practice that is not first and fundamentally in the best interest of the client? Treat your clients and prospects as you would desire to be treated when contracting for professional services. Doing so will pay off. It will produce a return that has both great economic and psychological advantage.

INDEX